The Secret To Answered Prayer

Six Essentials for Successful Prayer

Dr. Charles R. Vogan Jr., Ph.D.

Ravenbrook Publishers
PO Box 103
Weyers Cave, VA 24486

A subsidiary of
Shenandoah Bible Ministries

—————— ❦ ——————

www.shenbible.org

ISBN 978-0-6151-3864-0

1 2

Contents

INTRODUCTION

There have been so many studies done on the subject of prayer over the centuries that it would be foolish to presume that any one book could deal with prayer in all of its facets. It's bigger than any of us. For one thing, no single book can give us a fair idea of what it is like to stand before the Almighty and hold a conversation with him — which is exactly what prayer is. It is an experience that requires libraries to describe.

Hopefully this study doesn't make the mistake of assuming too much about itself. If you want to find out about prayer, get and read many books on the subject, because there are many good works that will bless your prayer experiences. Prayer should be your lifelong study, and as it says in Proverbs 15:22, the more counselors the better — the more that you can learn from the experiences of others in their prayers, the better you will pray.

But there does seem to be a gaping hole in the prayer experience of today's Church. When we read about Christians in history that, when they prayed, literally brought Heaven down to earth and great things happened as a result, we stand simply amazed. They seemed to understand what it takes to be heard in God's court, and their prayers got powerful results. Then in other ages (ours included) prayer has had more form than substance and not much happened when people prayed; in fact, they were actually afraid to ask for God's miracles because they didn't think that prayer would change anything, and they didn't want to be disappointed!

The difference is that successful prayer is grounded on some critical foundation stones, truths that give power and direction to prayer. The believer who finds out what these principles are, and uses them when he prays, will discover the God of the Bible who answers prayer in awesome and real ways. The believer who doesn't bother to examine whether his prayers are worth anything will just have to do without answers to his prayers.

And it's not as if these foundations were exotic mysteries never before revealed to men! They are simple truths, taught over and over again in many forms, through the entire Bible. God has been careful to teach them to all of his children so that they can come to him and get what they ask for. We really have no excuse for not being skilled in prayer. Our problem seems to be that we are slow to learn.

Perhaps you won't find your favorite aspect of prayer discussed here; but remember, this isn't an attempt to deal with every angle of the subject. You need to put this together with other studies on prayer if you want a full picture. But you at least must have these six things mastered if you want to get anywhere with God when you pray. They are plain and clear principles that the Lord teaches us in his Word. If you ignore them, then don't expect any answers from God when you pray. If you study them and form your prayers around them like flesh on a skeleton, your prayer time will come alive in the presence of God and you will begin to see answers to your prayers — which is what prayer is all about, after all.

ONE REASON FOR EXAMINING OUR PRAYERS

Our relationship with God is, without a doubt, the most amazing state of affairs in the entire universe. We were made "in God's image", which sets man apart from the rest of the creation in his nature and in his work. "While we were still sinners, Christ died for us" — this is the banner of the Christian Church: how important man must be that God's only Son died for his sake! "He gave [them] the right to become children of God" — who can fathom this! We alone of all created beings can come right up to God's throne and, holding his hands in adoration, speak directly to him as our father. God, in amazing mercy, has surely lifted his children up in high honor and privilege. The angels, as powerful and as privileged as they are, can only look on in wonder as we sinners move up from condemnation, to salvation, to adoption, and finally by God's grace to a position of ruling over the angels themselves.

But, like bad little children in the royal family, we sometimes forget the rules. We weren't saved in order to do whatever we like! If anything, our salvation was the beginning of a long learning experience in which we will find out what our Father is like, and what he expects of us if we are to please him. There is a great deal of training involved if we are going to be skillful "kings and priests" in his kingdom. "I urge you to live a life worthy of the calling you have received." (Ephesians 4: 1)

I'm afraid that we've taken our special relationship with God for granted. It's true that we are the "apple of his eye" and that we are destined for the throne at his right hand. But it is *not* true that we are now free to live as we please. And it's especially not true that we can worship God in whatever way we like. Even though we are family now, it's a grave and dangerous error to think that we can take liberties with our God. Remember the lesson that the sons of Aaron, who were priests like their father, learned when they decided they could worship God in their own way: they were immediately destroyed! And God didn't apologize for the rough treatment, either; instead he declared in anger that —

> Among those who approach me I will show myself holy; in the sight of all the people I will be honored. (Leviticus 10:3)

The Lord gave the Israelites a complex and extensive system of law that completely described how they were to worship him. He left nothing to guesswork. It was the most complete worship system ever practiced in history, because in it God himself described what it would take to properly honor him. There have been other systems of worship that were devised by man, but they all fall short of the goal; people may be completely devoted to a particular system of worship but that doesn't mean that they are getting anywhere with it! In God's eyes it is all wrong. His Law explains what has to be done and what is the proper way of going about it; which stands to reason, because it is him that we must please with our worship. We may as well find out from him what he expects from us!

New Testament Christians usually don't appreciate the solid foundation that this Law provides for our worship of the Father. It's true that we don't have to do much of what the Old Testament Law requires; but we need it nonetheless, because without it we will never please God. The difference between us and the early Israelites is that *they themselves* had to perform the necessary ceremony; with *us*, however, it is Jesus Christ who fulfills the Law's requirements for us. We get into the presence of God because Christ has fulfilled the duties and responsibilities of High Priest on our behalf. The Law of God still stands; it's just that Jesus is doing more for us right now than we realize.

What we are left with, in the meantime, is the relationship itself. While Christ does the necessary Law-work for us, he encourages us to take advantage of our closeness to God and begin relating to him as our God and Father. Jesus opens the veil between earth and Heaven, clothes us in pure robes of righteousness, teaches us what God is like, ushers us into God's presence, and bids us speak to our Father. That's all we have to do! At first we don't know what to say; we are overwhelmed by God's glory, and new to the things of God's kingdom. But the Spirit helps us by prompting our hearts with the appropriate things to ask of God.

It's a simple matter, and the reason that it's so simple is because of the massive amount of work that God did in Christ to make it all possible. But here we often make a serious mistake: we think that God will always be pleased with the childish babblings of our infancy. When we first meet God he accepts even the smallest seed of faith, the simplest prayer; but over a period of time he begins to get concerned when we don't show signs of *growing up*.

Prayer is the most important aspect of our relationship with God, because there is where we come close to him, and he to us, and this business of Christianity becomes more than so many words in a dusty Bible. We prove that there is a God when we pray to him and he speaks back to us. But, for as crucial a thing as prayer is for our spiritual well-being, it's the least practiced part of our Christian walk. This is so tragic. For some reason we think that the level of childish understanding that we had when we first became believers will do well enough for talking to God as we get older. It's as if a son never changed the way he addressed his father: instead of saying, "Dad, may I have the keys to the car tonight?" he would never get beyond "Dada, wawa!" We have so much to discuss with God, and we are learning a lot about God's ways and God's kingdom and the shallowness of this world, and the needs of our brothers and sisters seem to cry out all the louder as the years go on. If anything, our prayers should become more intense and sophisticated! We are God's "partners" in the work of the kingdom, and we have to hold high-level talks with him in wisdom and discernment and great faith.

Instead we hardly know what to say beyond "Please heal Aunt Matilda's toe, Lord!" What is worse, we often insult his intelligence and honor; the angels surely cringe when we pray, because they can see the Lord in his glory while we babble on about our opinions and our wishes and our glory in front of God. It's then that he positively gets angry.

Could we be doing something wrong? Are we afraid to ask that question? Or maybe we are too proud to ask it? Well, you needn't be afraid nor too proud to ask it because there is a simple test that you can apply to find out if God is taking your prayers seriously. It is this: does God answer you?

That seems unthinkable, that God wouldn't answer your prayers. Yet there are two unarguable facts that prove that such a thing is certainly possible: first, that *he said* he may not answer your prayers; and second, that you *may not be getting* any answers to your prayers. You can't very well argue with either one.

As for the first point, the Lord made it clear that there are certain circumstances in which he will refuse to listen to prayer; it will be no use to expect any answers.

> When you spread out your hands in prayers I will hide
> my eyes from you; even if you offer many prayers, I
> will not listen. (Isaiah 1:15)

It's hard to talk to God if he isn't listening; or should I say, it seems to be *too easy* to do that — perhaps because we aren't aware of the fact that he isn't paying any attention to us. We often don't have the spiritual discernment to know if God is listening to us pray. So we have expressions like, "My prayers don't seem to be getting any higher than the ceiling." They probably aren't. Not that we are always going to feel ecstatic highs when we pray successfully; but the normal practice, as we shall see later, is that we usually should be able to sense the presence of God when we pray. And if he isn't there, then we should be able to tell that too.

The second point is more obvious. If God doesn't answer us, that is a pretty good sign that he isn't listening. Conversation is a two-way street, remember, and it's pointless to talk to God if he isn't going to answer us. You may enjoy talking to yourself, but that isn't prayer. A writer once wondered what it would be like if God suddenly answered someone, point by point, as they prayed the Lord's prayer. He decided that the average person just may consider God's answers to be irritating interruptions during his time of "devotions"! It's odd, but we often pray according to formula and pattern without giving any thought at all to the fact that we are really after answers with all this. And when no answers come, we think that's normal!

But perhaps it is too painful a thought that we may be doing prayer all wrong. Maybe we have so much faith in God that we know he *is* always listening, and that answers aren't all that important. Just to pray is the important thing; if we do that, then it will all work out.

Then we meet someone like David who upsets our prim little world. Imagine the scene: here we are in God's throne room, praying in our own way and God reacting to us as he always does (that is, he probably isn't paying much attention to us), and then David comes into the room. Suddenly God's face lights up, he turns to greet David and draws him close, and motions angels away as if their business is much less important than this newcomer. He listens intently to David's words: he beams with joy at one thing, frowns with deep concern at another, and at one point jumps out of his throne in great anger. With seemingly little effort this man moves the heart of God this way and that. As we watch, we wish we knew God so well as to touch those inner springs of emotion and motivation as David can. When he is done, God orders his angels to equip David with treasure and weapon; he gives his orders to David, who nods quietly as he listens to God's secret counsel; he sends David back out to do the great and critical work that he has prepared for him. When David is gone, the Lord returns to us with a polite look but obviously his mind is on other matters.

You can't argue with success. David obviously captured God's attention when he prayed; when he cried for help, the Lord in anger hurled his wrath at David's enemies and lifted him up to a secure place (Psalm 18); when he pleaded for forgiveness, the Lord cleansed his heart and restored to him the "joy of salvation" (Psalm 51); when he needed wisdom, the Lord instructed him in his ways (Psalm 25). David prayed for answers; he didn't pray just to hear himself talk. And to see God answer his prayers convinces us that David was doing something right.

There are certain things that God likes to see in prayer. There aren't many things, and we needn't worry that he expects so much of us that we will be hopelessly lost in the complexity of trying to please him in every way. As we've already seen, Jesus has taken the complexity and the impossibility out of it for us — what we are left with is something within our capability. But we must at least do what he has given us! If we haven't learned this thing about God, then we must start here: that God is very particular about how someone approaches him.

A keen eye will see this trait of God in the Bible. Study the instructions of the ceremony of worship in Exodus and Leviticus; study the way the Temple was prepared for and built in David's and Solomon's time. If there is anything that we can definitely say about God in respect to worship it is that *he requires ceremony.* Ceremony may be a bad word to you, and often times it's a convenient replacement for true worship of the heart: people would rather go through formal ritual than meet God face to face! But in spite of the abuse of ceremony, it serves a critical role in true worship. By following the ceremony a person can be certain that he is doing the action correctly, as God wishes it to be done, and that he is saying the words as God wants them to be said. For example, the Church has a ceremony for two people getting married; if the ritual is followed closely then these two have indeed tied themselves together in responsibility and love for each other. The same is true of God's ceremonies: if a person follows them then he can be more certain of getting God's ear.

After all, God's ceremony isn't just an empty form. A Jew who had no eye for the things of God probably thought that some of those requirements in the Temple service were pretty useless; interesting, but not important in themselves. But a Jew "who was one inwardly" knew that these outward forms taught a spiritual reality. He knew that, in some way, each ceremony reflected an eternal truth in God's kingdom and it was vitally important for his salvation that he stick to that ceremony. In the same way, we may wonder why God expects us to pray a certain way; but we wonder only because we don't see the appropriateness of it. Once we learn who God really is, in his full glory, and learn what it's like to live in his world, then the ceremony becomes precious to us because it teaches and reminds us of God.

This is the heart of what it means to live with God in this world. Before we were converted we had no certain proof that God existed, and we really didn't care because he wasn't a part of our world. Now, however, we are awake to God and fully aware of him — at least we have that capability now, at any rate. We should live as if these things are real. Isn't that the definition of faith?

> Without faith it is impossible to please God, because anyone who comes to him must believe that he exists and that he rewards those who earnestly seek him. (Hebrews 11:6)

We know that these "rewards" that God has for his people are real things, things that this world can't match with its shallow hopes and promises. A Christian believes in these things! That's why unbelievers shake their heads over us -

> The man without the Spirit does not accept the things that come from the Spirit of God, for they are foolishness to him, and he cannot understand them, because they are spiritually discerned. (1 Corinthians 2:14)

Now — what do you think God feels like when his own people don't believe in such things? When he has said, over and over, that he is a consuming fire, why don't his people approach him in fear and thoroughly ashamed of their sins? When he has said that faith will move mountains, why aren't his people trusting him for miracles? When he has said that he is building a Church, why are his people so interested in everything else except what God is doing in his Church? When he has said that he will destroy the world and everything in it, why are his people so busy running after the things in this world and why are they not storing up the treasures that God has provided for them in Heaven? When Christians don't believe these things, what is God to do? Why should he answer prayers of such unforgivable unbelief?

So he won't. If we won't take him seriously, then he won't take us seriously. If we don't think that his world is real, then he won't give any of it to us. If we are so content to live our lives here, then he won't give us a foretaste of life there with him. If we insist on doing things our own way, then he won't do them for us. The result is that we go begging and there are no answers for us.

We are all too familiar with life without answers to prayer. We say that God answers our prayers, but really we have gotten so used to living without answers that we've talked ourselves into thinking that such a mediocre existence is actually the result of prayer. Instead of victory over sin, we struggle with and often lose to the sins in our hearts. Instead of unity, the people of God constantly find new reasons for not getting along with each other. Instead of being a good influence on the world, the world is twisting our lives into conformity with *its* standards. We are afraid of things around us; we have no comforter to guide us; we have no wisdom, no insight, about what ought to be done in the present circumstances. These are the marks of a person who is on his own in this world — we can hardly say that such a person is getting answers to prayers. And we will inevitably find, when we get to the bottom of it all, that the person who lives such a life isn't praying for any specific answer from God, as well as praying in the wrong manner. Because if we can't get a hold of the eternal realities of God in our prayers, and ask for the concrete and real things of Heaven, then it's no wonder that we never see them in our lives.

But what is life like when God answers our prayers? It's just the opposite of the above! It's like a spring day after a long winter. It's like an army riding in and freeing the city. It's like a new love. Things change when God shows up; he lowers mountains and raises up valleys. He comes to —

> . . . preach good news to the poor. He has sent me to proclaim freedom for the prisoners and recovery of sight for the blind, to release the oppressed, to proclaim the year of the Lord's favor. (Luke 4:18-19)

What a day of rejoicing! Peter once asked, when he looked at the reality of this world, whether there was any hope at all of the promises of God happening. Jesus answered that "all things are possible with God." (Matthew 10:27) You just don't know the hope and joy and peace that are possible until God actually comes down to answer your prayers. You would be amazed at how he can bring so much light out of so much darkness.

I call on you, O God, for you will answer me; give ear to me and hear my prayer. (Psalm 17:6)

What makes the difference in prayer? What is the secret that gets answers from God? It's all in *how* you pray.

PRAY ACCORDING TO HIS WORD

Do good to your servant according to your Word, O LORD.
(Psalm 119:65)

Imagine that you are at a typical prayer meeting. As you and others gather around and sit down, you decide to watch and listen this time — you want to see how the typical Christian comes to God in prayer. There are some preliminary remarks, someone organizes who will pray for specific "needs", and then the room gets quiet as each person bows his/her head. Before you close your eyes you notice that nobody has a Bible along.

People pray spontaneously, here and there, bringing up concerns that are on their hearts. The topics range from some general remarks about appreciating the privilege of getting together and praying, to health concerns, to financial crises in someone's life, and perhaps more general remarks about the ministry of the church. Most requests are that God would "bless" this person and that ministry, that God's Word would go out in power and "bless" the people.

When the time has come to end the session, the leader will wind up with his own general requests and finally end the prayer with "In Jesus' name, Amen." There are some sighs, people start moving around, and conversation picks up. The prayer meeting is over and everyone goes home.

Does this sound familiar to you? Most prayer meetings follow this format with a few variations here and there. Aside from the fact that they are suffering from spiritual anemia, and they can't expect to get concrete answers when they don't ask for anything specific, the common denominator across almost all modern-day prayer meetings is that nobody carries a Bible along. We will look later at some of the other symptoms of spiritual sickness in this typical prayer meeting, but now we want to focus on perhaps the root cause of all their impotence in prayer: they don't pray according to God's Word.

This isn't an ailment of only group prayer meetings. Individual Christians suffer from the same illness; it is a rare Christian who will even hold a Bible, let alone look inside one, when he is praying.

This is all the more remarkable when we consider that the Bible is perhaps the primary symbol of evangelical Christianity. Centuries ago the Protestants broke from the Catholic Church around this very issue: we have the right, they stoutly declared, to read God's Word for ourselves instead of relying on a priest's intercession for us. And from that day to this, the evangelical Church has printed the Bible in hundreds of languages so that millions of people everywhere can have their own copy and read it for themselves. We rich Americans usually have many copies on our shelves. We are "the people of the book" and we fought for that right. We use the words of the Bible in our schools, in our debates, in our politics, on our national money; we fill bookstores all around the nation with thousands of titles that help us understand the Bible better. We listen to sermons and lessons that teach us what the Bible says. If someone would take the Bible out of our lives altogether, we would be without a religion.

Yet when we pray, we act as if there is no Bible. We usually don't even think about using it for prayer. If prayer is our contact with God, and the most important avenue that we have for getting in touch with God, why in the world do we leave our most important resource for that contact at home? Why is the Bible good for everything else *except* prayer?

Christians need a great deal of training when it comes to prayer, and the starting place for their training has to be the Bible. And we certainly get a lot of instruction about the Bible from various church activities and books and conversations with other believers. One would think that some of this would seep into our prayers by osmosis; surely if we learn God's Scriptures by heart, we will pray accordingly.

But that isn't necessarily so. The Bible is a spiritual book, not a natural one, and if someone hopes to understand the message there then he needs insight that the Holy Spirit gives. We can learn its verses by rote and never see the truth in it. People do it all the time! So when they pray, they may *sound* like they have been reading the Bible, but they really don't have a spiritual understanding of what they are talking about. And of course God knows the problem that they have; he isn't fooled by appearances as we are.

What we want to do now is to look at why the Bible simply has to be the starting point for all your prayers. You must pray according to God's Word if you want him to answer you. In fact, Jesus commanded us to pray according to his Word: "His worshipers must worship in Spirit and *in Truth*." (John 4:24)

WHAT IS GOD'S WORD FOR?

Perhaps we first need to review the purpose of God's Word. If we know why he gave it to us, and how he wants us to use it, then that will give us a good start for praying in a way that pleases him.

- *God's Word reveals.* The Word of God is the "revelation" of God, which means that, unless we read it, we will have no idea at all what God is really like. It shows us who he is, whereas no other source can even pretend to teach us about him. All books and teachers have to get their information about God straight from the Bible if they want to teach the truth. And nobody can claim to know the true God unless they learned of him from the Scriptures; all other gods, no matter how true to life they sound, are false gods.

    God's world is hidden from us like the inside of a shuttered house. There are several reasons why we don't know anything about him — our sin, the darkness we were born in, the fact that God hides himself from us, the deceit of the enemy, the false appearances in this world — but the fact of the matter is, he is a mystery to us. We could never find out the truth about him on our own; you can see that clearly enough from the struggles of men and schools throughout history as they tried to peer out beyond this world into God's kingdom. Their theories and systems all contradict each other! How can any of them possibly be right when they don't account for all the facts involved?

Furthermore, man *can't* understand the things of God, not without Divine help. He isn't able to see God and know him. God presented himself in many times and various ways to all sorts of people in history, and many times the people present were dumbfounded — they had no idea how to interpret what their eyes saw and their ears heard.

So the purpose of the Bible is to inform us about what we can't see and teach us about the God beyond this world. It's news from Heaven; it lays out new facts before us that we can't get from any other source. If this was all it was, however, people still wouldn't understand it because they can't understand without the help of the Spirit of God, which we will see later. For now, though, we need to get our facts straight about him, and nobody else has been able to help us in this matter like the Bible can.

• ***God's Word is the truth.*** "What is truth?" Pilate asked Jesus. He suffered from the same mental exhaustion that we all have — there are so many ways of looking at things, and apparently contradictory theories are often both true, to some extent, and the most promising philosophies turn out to be hollow shams in the end. Around and around we go looking for something that we can hang our hats on, something that completely and correctly describes life and it can't be changed or challenged. We haven't found anything yet, except perhaps we have faith only in ourselves now.

Well, look no further. The Bible is *the Way* of looking at things. In this book there are no two ways of looking at something; God has an opinion about everything, and he recorded his opinion in his Word so that we too will look at every matter as he does.

Of course there are a million angles to everything in life; there is always a special interest group who will challenge the traditional ways of doing things and try to introduce new ideas and new ways that they claim will improve things. Our society is so used to this happening that now we are afraid we might be offending someone with our beliefs, afraid that someone is going to challenge us and force us to give up our beliefs — that is the rule now rather than the exception. Our world is in an upheaval because nobody knows what to believe anymore. One group says that one thing is right, and another says that it's wrong. The accuser says that he was wronged by the defendant, and the defendant claims he was the one wronged. Are they both right?

But the Bible cuts a path through the maze of opinions with one opinion — God's opinion — and it doesn't care how offended people may get with it. It makes the claim that God's truth is *the* truth, that it has the truth, and that all men everywhere are obligated to learn and live by this truth alone. It even threatens judgment against whoever rejects its truth.

• ***God's Word is what God intends to do.*** If God would just stay up there in Heaven and not bother us, a lot of people would be more comfortable about him. In fact, the study of God would become quite interesting: a philosophical challenge, doctrinal case studies, a subject of interesting discussion at the dinner table and in polite society.

But he is *not* going to stay up there. God is on the move. He has already made several assaults on our rebellious planet in the past, sometimes in person and sometimes with armies of angels; and once he came in his Son and dealt his enemy a death blow that sent him sprawling in the dust. But he isn't done yet. He intends to keep coming at us, sending more angels and sending his Spirit, assaulting the strongholds of the world and tearing down all resistance to him. He intends to come to *us*, too, and do things that perhaps we will fear. He will keep coming and coming and coming — until he does *all* his will.

Now if we were completely in the dark about his plans and what he keeps coming to do in our lives, we would certainly resist him whenever we see him and we would be afraid of his mysterious presence. But the Bible tells us clearly what God wants to do in our lives, and how and when he will do those things. He lets us know ahead of time in his Word. It's as if we were able to read his daily schedule in the morning, *before* he got started.

God is not an inactive God, nor does he have any intentions of letting us go our own way. One of the important reasons that he had for giving us his Word is to let us know that he fully intends to finish the creation that he started thousands of years ago. He has definite plans in store for it; his plans for finishing the job are as detailed as the ones he used to create it. We can see in the Bible the construction site, as it were, with his tools lying about and the workmen getting ready to do the job and the blueprints for the finished product. It's a precious blessing to have such insight into the works of God.

USING GOD'S WORD IN PRAYER

As you can see, the Word of God is more than just a book of interesting facts about God, or even a resource of religious doctrines for Christians. It's a world view, a way of living, an open door into God's world where things don't work or look like things do here in this world. It is light, and therefore important to us as light is important. Without light we can't see what is around us, and without light we will inevitably end up in serious trouble — our enemies have the advantage when we can't see what we're doing. So the Bible is a life-saving source of truth. We would do well to *think* about the truth in it.

And nowhere does the special nature of the Bible get proven so well as in prayer. If we have shallow prayers, it shows that we have a shallow understanding of the Word. If the God we pray to is weak and helpless and can't do much for us, then that shows how little we know about God after reading the Bible. Our prayers are a barometer of our understanding of the Word: if we understand little of it, we pray ignorantly; if we understand it very well, we pray like a master.

The great men and women of the past who prayed well, knew their Bibles inside and out. They were experts in the Word of God; they studied God's thoughts thoroughly; they knew how God does things, and what his kingdom is like, and the differences between this world and the next. They didn't all get their "great learning" from universities and books written by men, though through God's providence some of them learned truth from other spiritual masters. They all, however, could sit down with the Bible and explain to you anything you wanted to know about God; this was *their* book, they felt at home with it because they knew it so well. These saints weren't just knowledgeable about chapter and verse and able to quote any reference from memory; memorization of verses may or may not be a strength of yours and it certainly isn't necessary. What they *were* experts in is the truth that it taught. They lived this; they thought the same way that God thinks; they valued what he valued. It's no wonder that their prayers moved Heaven and earth.

John Bunyan, an uneducated preacher of the seventeenth century and author of **Pilgrim's Progress**, used to pray like this: he would go up into his attic at home, open up his Bible on a chair, get on his knees in front of it, and pray over its words page by page. He studied what God's Word meant, line by line, and then prayed that God would make this truth real in his life. He got answers. He was known as one of the most powerful preachers in England, and men with decades of learning under their belts sat under his ministry spellbound. Hundreds of people under his ministry were converted and many thousands of Christians were taught and encouraged as he doled out the treasures of Heaven. Bunyan knew how to get God's ear when he prayed — he started by opening his Bible.

There are four reasons why the Bible is so important for prayer:

• *The truth about God and his kingdom.* "You diligently study the Scriptures because you think that by them you possess eternal life. These are the Scriptures that testify about me, yet you refuse to come to me to have life." (John 5:39)

Not everybody understands what the Bible really teaches about God. But some do see him there in its pages, because they have "eyes to see and ears to hear" God speaking in his Word. To them the Bible is a window into God's world. They know who he is, whereas others can only talk about him.

The Bible is a guidebook for God's kingdom. When someone goes to another country he usually buys a tourist's guide before he goes, so that he won't be completely in the dark when he arrives in the strange land. It will teach him something about their customs and their language, and about the industry and education that he will find there, and the important places to see. In fact, if he wants to get anything out of his trip he would be foolish not to buy the book! He will find that he will come to depend on this little book for everything while he is there.

In the same way the Bible is our guide while we pray — which is another way of saying, when we take a trip into God's world. It teaches us the way people talk in his kingdom, and how they dress there; and it points out places of interest and shows us how we can get the most out of them. It reveals, in other words, the things of God so that we can become familiar with this strange new world. Heaven is so unlike earth that we need all the information about it that we can get. Praying without the Bible is like going overseas with no idea of what to do; it's closing one's eyes while in Heaven, and you can't expect to get anything from God if you refuse to look at him. There is too much that you will miss if you don't first study what to look for there; and when you come back from prayer, you will be like the traveler who came back home with no stories, no souvenirs, no memories, and having accomplished nothing by the trip.

There's another service that the Bible provides for us; it prevents idolatry. Since the beginning of the world, men have known that there is a God, and that they are obligated to him in some way. The problem has always been that they didn't know what he was like. They couldn't run the risk of ignoring him, so they did their best at inventing stories of what they imagined him to be like and worshipped that. That's the definition of idolatry. Whether or not they had stone or wood images to represent him doesn't matter; they made up a story of what he is like, and therefore their "God" was a false god. The world is still filled with idolaters, both civilized and uncivilized, who make up stories and worship false gods.

The Bible, however, gives us a true and dependable picture of God. We can know exactly what to expect when we come to him; we know what he will say and do to us. If we can love the God of the Bible then we can pray to him and we can find him in prayer; but if the God of the Bible makes us uncomfortable then at least we know not to pray to him! He is so different than all the false gods that men make up, that we will have no problem finding out who he really is. The Scriptures are very plain about him, and there is no confusion about him if you will just read what it says.

The problem is that people don't first check in the Bible to see what God is and does. They blunder into the throne room with their eyes closed, blabbering about this wish and that wish, demanding that God give them what they want in the way that they want it. If they would just open their eyes and see God, and listen to the Spirit as he teaches about him from the Word, then much if not all of what they will say to him will be completely different. The angels, I'm sure, are ashamed when they watch us ignorant creatures boldly approach the Almighty with little understanding of his glory. They know him, because they see him and they always stand before his throne to serve him. Imagine their shock when they see little humans *demanding* that God bend his will around theirs! Obviously, the angels think to themselves, this creature doesn't understand the One they are addressing.

There are certain things that God will do and there are things that he won't do. Don't you think that we should know about all that beforehand, before we go to him and start demanding what we want? The Bible tells us not only what God has done in the past (which is a clue about what we can expect him to do again) but what he intends to do now and in the future. It tells us how God does things. He has a certain way of going about his business (which, by the way, almost always bothers us — our ways are completely different than his and we can't understand how God expects to get his will done by the ways he chooses to do it) and we need to know those ways if we hope to fit in with his work.

For example, the Word teaches us that he won't do anything — even if you pray for it — that will allow you to sin. He won't do anything that will give you the glory for something instead of him. He is interested in building up his spiritual Temple, so you may as well focus on that when you pray. He intends to save you from sin and death, so you should get in step with his will for your life. These are just a few samples of the knowledge of God, and they serve to guide your prayers to the right end.

The Bible does one more thing for us in respect to prayer — it teaches us about the things in Heaven. We know what the treasures in this world are, because we've lived here all our lives. We also know that there isn't anything here worth living for; God has already passed judgment on the whole thing and he intends to "burn it up" at the last day once it has served his purpose. But the things of Heaven are different: they are eternal, never-ending, solid. We can base our lives on these things. And the Lord wants us to start thinking about his kingdom now, before we get there, and start planning for our inheritance now. He wants us to learn what those treasures are and why they are valuable to us. He wants us to begin praying about them now.

> Since, then, you have been raised with Christ, set your hearts on things above, where Christ is seated at the right hand of God. Set your minds on things above, not on earthly things. (Colossians 3:1-2)

> Do not store up for yourselves treasures on earth, where moth and rust destroy, and where thieves break in and steal. But store up for yourselves treasures in Heaven, where moth and rust do not destroy, and where thieves do not break in and steal. For where your treasure is, there your heart will be also. (Matthew 6:19-21)

These are your inheritance, child of God! Do you value these things more than what you own in this world? Or do you even know what the treasures in Heaven are? Moses knew; the Bible tells us that "he regarded disgrace for the sake of Christ as of greater value than the treasures of Egypt, because he was looking ahead to his reward." (Hebrews 11:26) Almost everyone prays, but only a very few pray for God's treasures in Heaven. We show our spiritual-mindedness when we know the right thing to ask for, just as Solomon showed how good a king he was going to be when he asked God for wisdom to rule the people instead of worldly wealth. (2 Chronicles 1:7-12)

• *The truth about ourselves.*   "Sharper than any double-edged sword, it penetrates even to dividing soul and spirit, joints and marrow; it judges the thoughts and attitudes of the heart." (Hebrews 4:12) God isn't done when he has revealed *himself* in his Word; he has a word to say about *us* too. We may think that we know all about ourselves — who would know a man better than himself? — but God disagrees. He can see into our hearts where we can't see (or won't look) and describe our natures as we really are.

When we compare our notes with his, the difference is really embarrassing. We are too prone to cover over some areas in our lives and hold other areas out for people to see; God, however, uncovers things about us that we'd rather he didn't get into. We want everyone to see our works and our nice side; God drags out our bad side for public view, and he smashes our works like so much worthless pottery. There have been all sorts of studies and explanations of what man is, but none of them agree with God's analysis. Whereas we think that man has a lot of potential, he's got a dim view of man the sinner:

> The Lord saw how great man's wickedness on
> the earth had become, and that every inclination
> of the thoughts of his heart was only evil all the
> time. (Genesis 6:5)

Man in general has a lot about him that God wants to change. The Scriptures are pretty plain about what we are and what we need to be. For instance, here is what God sees when he looks down on men everywhere in the world:

> There is no one righteous, not even one;
>   there is no one who understands,
>   no one who seeks God.
> All have turned away,
>   they have together become worthless;

there is no one who does good,
not even one.
Their throats are open graves;
their tongues practice deceit.
The poison of vipers is on their lips.
Their mouths are full of cursing and bitterness.
Their feet are swift to shed blood;
ruin and misery mark their ways,
and the way of peace they do not know.
There is no fear of God before their eyes.
(Romans 3:10-18)

That's a pretty grim description of humanity, but we can't question the fact that this is what God sees in people. Of course *they* don't see this; they are all busy justifying themselves and proving that they are good — by their own standards. But as Paul says in this passage, the standard has to be *God's* Law, not man's, because God accurately describes what he sees.

Prayer, then, has to address these issues first. One must realize, when he comes to God in prayer, that he is part of this group of sinners that God sees on earth. Just keeping that in mind will give us the correct attitude when we approach the Holy One.

Second, the Bible deals not only with mankind in general but with *you* in particular. This book has an uncanny way of putting its finger on where we live. Just when we were feeling pretty smug about our self-righteousness, we read a passage that strikes a sword through our hearts with conviction. For example, who hasn't read this verse and cringed at what it knows about our thoughts?

You have heard that it was said. "Do not commit adultery." But I tell you that anyone who looks at a woman lustfully has already committed adultery with her in his heart. (Matthew 5:27-28)

We find that the Bible knows us all too well. Many people prefer not to read it for that very reason: we find that it is too painful to be exposed to God's scrutiny like that. We don't like to face the truth about ourselves. In fact, many Christians have developed the ability to read the Bible without letting down their guard against it — they can read the very words that condemn them and not see the point!

But the prayer that God listens to is a prayer of brokenness before the Word of God. When David was faced with his sin, when he listened to God's Word and took it to heart, he realized then that God would hear his cry for forgiveness:

> The sacrifices of God are a broken spirit; a broken and contrite heart, O God, you will not despise. (Psalm 51:17)

In the hands of the Spirit the Bible is an accurate diagnosis of our spiritual condition. Listen to it. It will point out your problem areas, the sins that you have to get rid of, the weak spots in your character that you have to strengthen. It will tell you what you need to be doing in order to be a more productive Christian. It has all the answers for your problems; it will even anticipate your objections and answer those. The Bible is a phenomenal book — surely it does come from God because it describes each of us so well.

But there is even more that the Bible does for us — it describes the "perfect man", the goal that we should all be striving for. This is what a praying man is, it tells us; here is a man of faith; here is what obedience looks like. We don't have to wonder what it will take to please God nor do we have to wonder if we have reached that goal. If your life looks like Christ's life, then you've reached the goal that God has for you. If it doesn't, then you have a great deal to pray about.

• *Matters to deal with.* "All Scripture is God-breathed and is useful for teaching, rebuking, correcting and training in righteousness, so that the man of God may be thoroughly equipped for every good work." (2 Timothy 3:16)

How do you know what to pray about? Do you keep a list of things to pray over? Some people do, but others simply wait until the time for prayer and then say whatever pops into their heads. Since they don't really have an agenda, their prayers turn into a general mishmash of wishes and feelings but nothing really specific and no burning issues.

Well, that's the purpose of the Bible. God doesn't want us to show up before his throne with mishmash. We are partners with him in the building of his kingdom; we aren't to remain little children in our thinking and our ways. We are supposed to be grappling with great issues! Our hearts should burn with shame over our sin. The glory of God should be shining in our eyes, causing us to fall down before him in adoration and worship. Our minds should be constantly searching for solutions to the spiritual problems around us. We should be making plans for our move to Heaven. We should be in training for the war against our enemies. If all this is true of you when you pray, then you don't need to be told what to pray about. But if, instead, you are occupied with lining your own little nest during your stay in this world and you want God to be your bellboy, going for this and that, to "bless" you, then it's about time you opened your Bible and learned what God wants you to be praying about.

Prayer is sort of like a meat grinder. You can turn the handle all you want, but unless you put meat into the top of the grinder you will never get sausage out the side. It needs something to work on. So it is with prayer — it needs good material to work on if it is going to produce the desired results. If you want poor answers, keep feeding your prayers with whatever comes into your head; but if you want answers that will change your life, pour the Word of God into your prayers.

There is much to grind on — I mean pray over in this book. David found a lot to chew on, literally, in God's Word: "But his delight is in the Law of the LORD, and on his Law he meditates day and night." (Psalm 1:2) Meditating on the Word of God is like what a cow does when she chews her cud — a very picturesque way of using the Bible! And when you do "chew on" what the Bible is saying, it won't take long till you start seeing what God considers important enough to start praying for.

He has priorities in his kingdom which he explains very carefully in his Word. What *he* thinks is important won't necessarily be what *you* think is important, but then he isn't running this universe to please you and me. He is perfectly willing to postpone, or even cancel, those things that *we* want to see happen right away. He insists on steam-rolling other issues through, however, when we are reluctant to cooperate with him. Hopefully the Spirit of grace will work in our hearts so that we will start changing our priorities to fit in with his. It will take grace before we will, though, because our rebellion and self-centeredness dies hard.

What are these priorities that he wants us to pray about? They are strewn throughout the Bible.

Only be careful, and watch yourselves closely so that you do not forget the things your eyes have seen or let them slip from your heart as long as you live. Teach them to your children and to their children after them. (Deuteronomy 4:9)

LORD, who may dwell in your sanctuary? Who may live on your holy hill? He whose walk is blameless and who does what is righteous, who speaks the truth from his heart and has no slander on his tongue . . . (Psalm 15)

Let love and faithfulness never leave you; bind them around your neck, write them on the tablet of your heart. Then you will win favor and a good name in the sight of God and man. (Proverbs 3:3-4)

LORD, I have heard of your fame; I stand in awe of your deeds, O LORD. Renew them in our day, in our time make them known; in wrath remember mercy. (Habakkuk 3:2)

He has showed you, O man, what is good. And what does the LORD require of you? To act justly and to love mercy and to walk humbly with your God. (Micah 6:8)

Love the Lord your God with all your heart and with all your soul and with all your mind. This is the first and greatest commandment. And the second is like it. Love your neighbor as yourself. All the Law and the Prophets hang on these two commandments. (Matthew 22:37-39)

Therefore, as God's chosen people, holy and dearly beloved, clothe yourselves with compassion, kindness, humility, gentleness and patience. Bear with each other and forgive whatever grievances you may have against one another. Forgive as the Lord forgave you. And over all these virtues put on love, which binds them all together in perfect unity. (Colossians 3:12-14)

These are the kinds of things that God considers important. In fact, as far as he is concerned, other matters can be put on the shelf for the time being while you attend to these issues first. You can lose life and health and friends and family and job and security and still get into Heaven in the end — if you are careful to do the things that God wants you to do. Skip these, though, and nothing you own or are will save you.

You are God's servant. A servant reports to his master to find out his orders for the day. When you pray, your attitude should be like this — you should be concerned to get God's orders for your life so that you can obey him and please him. That will happen only if you have your Bible open and you are pleading with him to make his will known to you through his Truth. "Your kingdom come, your will be done, on earth as it is in Heaven." (Matthew 6:10) He is King, and he has spoken to us, so his Word is his will for our lives.

• *Claims on his promise.* "My eyes stay open through the watches of the night, that I may meditate on your promises." (Psalm 119:148)

A fourth and very important way to use the Bible in prayer is to claim God's promises. He really committed himself to us a long time ago, in various promises and covenants, and he is still committed to us. "Because God wanted to make the unchanging nature of his purpose very clear to the heirs of what was promised he confirmed it with an oath." (Hebrews 6:17) Heaven and earth may pass away, but his promises to his children will stand forever in their original form. God fully intends to do good to all of his people.

Most of us know the promises of God perhaps better than anything else in the Bible. Some people carry Scripture verses in their pockets with a promise written on it, like a promise-a-day kind of thing. These are the good things of Christianity! And we ask God for these promises in our prayers.

But do we really understand these promises? Let's take one for an example: the promise of salvation. When we explore this idea in the Bible, here is what we find:

He is going to save us from sin — not from ill-treatment or hunger or bad grades or poverty or other physical setbacks. And we *need* to be saved; we are eaten up with sin.

God will do the saving; it isn't up to us to save ourselves. He alone knows what needs to be done, and he alone can save us. If it were up to us, we would neither be able to save ourselves nor would we want to.

God will save us over time. He doesn't take us right out of the world when we are first converted; conversion is the beginning of a process in which he gradually makes us into the image of Christ.

God will save us in his own way. We won't necessarily like how he does it; it will seem like hardship, but he is treating us as sons when he makes us hurt — it is for our good.

God will use the Spirit to save us — this is called sanctification. He will deal with us on a spiritual level, applying spiritual remedies to our lives and lifting us up into the spiritual realm of God's kingdom. Anything less than this isn't salvation.

There's more, but hopefully you get the point. This seemingly simple promise of God for salvation is a huge subject. There are large and important sections of the Bible entirely devoted to it. So you can't just use the word "salvation" with your own meaning attached; you can't pray "Lord save me" and not plead for the Biblical doctrine of salvation. If you are going to use the word, find out what it means in the Bible and then ask for *that* in your prayers. You will find that all of God's promises are like this — they are far bigger in scope than you realized. If nothing else, you will learn something new every time that you study about them.

The promises that God made to us are precious to him; he has been looking forward to fulfilling every one of these promises. Imagine his disappointment when we consider his promises of little importance! When we don't focus on them in prayer, we only show our apathy toward them. As if there is anything else in this world more important than what God's Word promises us! We ought to have these "great and precious promises" memorized by now, and rehearsing them over and over so that we will know exactly how to present our requests to God. Didn't Jesus say that our prayers ought to be like this?

> Then Jesus told his disciples a parable to show them that they should always pray and not give up . . . "And will not God bring about justice for his chosen ones, who cry out to him day and night? Will he keep putting them off? I tell you, he will see that they get justice, and quickly. However, when the Son of Man comes, will he find faith on the earth?" (Luke 18:1,7-8)

You actually honor him when you claim his promises. First of all, you are telling him that you have studied his Word and, as far as you are concerned, this is the truth — his Word is your hope. Second, you are coming to him to fulfill his Word. Prayer is simply bringing the truth of God back to him and asking him to do it for you. Sinners don't want to pray because they want nothing from God, but Christians pray because they want God to do everything for them. This lifts up the Name of God where it ought to be — the Name above all names, the Provider and Savior and everything else that we need from him. He gets glory when we pray for the fulfillment of his promises.

IF YOU DON'T USE IT . . .

It's sad but true that most people don't use their Bibles when they pray. Now I'm not saying that you must always have the book in your hands during your prayers; Paul says to "pray without ceasing" and a lot of times we have to pray when it isn't very handy to open a Bible. But there is such a thing as knowing the Bible so well that we will hold God's Word up to him when we pray, whether or not we have the printed page before us. The problem is that most of us don't know it very well at all, and it's hard to think of a text to pray over when we don't have the book open.

So, most of prayer is done without his Word — it is neither physically present nor is it present in our minds and hearts. What is disturbing is that people are actually comfortable about that! It doesn't bother them that they can pray without ever giving thought to whether or not they are praying "in truth." They are used to doing without the Bible; they don't even think about using it; they jump immediately into prayer with their own thoughts, not God's; they join hands with others and never wonder whether what is said is what God wants to hear.

There is a penalty to be paid for an attitude like that. If God has commanded that you worship him "in truth" then you can hardly expect to get anywhere with him by ignoring his Truth. "Your Word is truth." (John 17:17) When you pray without God's Word, this is what you should expect:

> • *You won't get any answers from God.* "So is my Word that goes out from my mouth: it will not return to me empty, but will accomplish what I desire and achieve the purpose for which I sent it." (Isaiah 55:11) This is what to expect from God's Word — results, answers. Whenever prayer is founded upon the Bible, you can

expect spiritual fruitfulness. But without his Word you can expect nothing to happen.

God blesses someone when they understand his truth and claim it for their lives. But if a person makes up what he wants from God, without any consideration of what the Bible says God will do, they shouldn't expect God to answer them. It's like planting a seed in salt and expecting it to grow. The package said to put it in good soil, not salt! It said to water it and fertilize it. It said to trim the bad branches. It told you what and how much to expect of this plant when full-grown. If you ignore the package instructions (the packagers know what they are talking about!) then you can hardly expect the seed to do anything. In the same way, if you ignore the written instructions in the Word of God and pray in the way that seems best to you, you are defying God's authority and putting yourself outside of his care.

Remember the parable of the seed that fell on the path? The Word came to some who paid no attention to it. They didn't listen, they didn't think about it, they didn't come back to God with it in their hands asking for what it promised — therefore they didn't profit by it. The enemy came along and removed God's Word from their lives (he has many ways of doing that, sometimes even by allowing us to continue using the Bible but without understanding it and being saved by it) and they remained the stony, hard path that they were before God spoke to them.

God promises to bless the work of his Word. If the Bible doesn't become the foundation of your life, don't expect his blessing.

• *Someone else may answer you.* "Why is my language not clear to you? Because you are unable to hear what I say. You belong to your father, the devil, and you want to carry out your father's desire. He was a murderer from the beginning, not holding to the truth, for there is no truth in him." (John 8:43-44) The main characteristic of the devil is that he does not respect God's Truth. And if you insist on praying without God's Word as a sure and safe guide, you run the great risk of getting someone interested in you who wants to make sure that you stay away from God's Word.

The devil is busy working in our world, and most Christians believe that; but what they may not realize is the *nature* of the work that the devil is doing here. Satan's primary work is to spread lies in order to counteract God's Truth. That's why the Bible is so critical for our spiritual well-being. The enemy's lies are often just a slight deviation from the truth; it's enough for his purposes that we believe most of what the Bible says if we will also believe a little of his untruth mixed in with it.

You don't want to be part of that, not if you love God. But how can you be sure that God will listen to you if you don't pray "in truth?" And if you don't pray according to the Truth, how can you expect not to strengthen Satan's hand in the world? Remember, we are at war — aiding the enemy is an act of treason! When you pray for *your* will, the devil will try to see to it that your will, not God's, is done. When you pray for things in this world, the devil will use his servants to give you the things of this world — so that the things of God won't become part of your life. He has the power to answer people's misguided prayers! He is "the ruler of the kingdom of the air, the spirit who is now at work in those who are disobedient." (Ephesians 2:2) Don't think that he will keep his hands off you simply because you claim God's Name; you have to work to stay close to God and frustrate the enemy's plans. Paul says that we have to do things God's way, "in order that Satan might not outwit us. For we are not unaware of his schemes." (2 Corinthians 2:11) Even the best of us are subject to the devil's whispering in our ears; Peter himself served the devil's purposes, and Jesus rebuked him for it. (Mark 8:33)

• *You dishonor God.* "'You are right in saying I am a king. In fact, for this reason I was born, and for this I came into the world, to testify to the truth. Everyone on the side of truth listens to me.' 'What is truth?' Pilate asked." (John 18:37-38) Pilate couldn't see the glory of Christ because he didn't know the truth about him; to Pilate, truth was whatever worked and it was constantly shifting according to his own needs and desires. He didn't see that truth is unchanging because it is God's viewpoint on things, and he didn't see that God's truth will save us from our biggest problems. Therefore, because he didn't know the truth, he despised this one who came to give us truth.

It's a shame, but people still despise Christ. They don't take his Word seriously, they don't think that he knows them better than they know themselves, they don't think he has the right or the ability to rule over them, and they don't think he has better things for them than what they have in mind for themselves. They dishonor him. He is, in fact, their Lord — he has the right to rule over them in all things. He is the Savior — he rescues from death, and pulls us away from what will kill our souls. He is the great High Priest — his ministry draws us close to God. If anybody knows what he is doing, Christ does! So when he speaks, he understandably expects people to listen and to do exactly what he says; there is life in his Word.

But when we pray without taking his Word seriously, we dishonor him. We are saying to him and to the world that what he tells us to pray about isn't worth our time and effort to look up. We are saying that his agenda for prayer isn't as important as our own. We are saying that we know better than he does how to conduct ourselves before the throne of grace. We are saying, "Not *your* will, but *my* will, be done" — and we say this to the Lord of Lords! You can hardly expect him to be pleased with you if you pray with an attitude like that. You are simply slapping him in the face in front of all the angels and saints in Heaven.

I hope that these three points bother you. I'm sure that you would never consciously pray to this end, to open yourself up to evil forces and purposely dishonor the Lord. I'm sure that you want to pray so that God would answer you with his blessings. But the fact remains that any of these unthinkable consequences are entirely possible even to the children of God. If you do something the wrong way, you can't expect good results, no matter what you call yourself. Even though we claim to be God's people (and perhaps we have good reason for it) we aren't immune from sin yet, not on this side of the grave. "*My people are destroyed from lack of knowledge.*" (Hosea 4:6) And it's a double shame if we sin against God in the very act of prayer, which is supposed to be the means of cleansing us from sin and honoring him.

AN EXAMPLE PRAYER

Believers in Bible times knew how to use God's Word when they prayed. They didn't have the entire Bible that we have, but they had his Word in some form or another and they clutched it in their hearts when they talked to God. These were important things to them, and they wanted these things from their God.

The disciples had the Old Testament Scriptures and they used them freely when praying. In Acts 4 we find a perfect example of how they used the Bible when they prayed. Here is the entire prayer:

Sovereign Lord, you made the Heavens and the earth and the sea, and everything in them. You spoke by the Holy Spirit through the mouth of your servant, our father David:

Why do the nations rage and the peoples plot in vain? The kings of the earth take their stand and the rulers gather together against the Lord and against his Anointed One.

Indeed Herod and Pontius Pilate met together with the Gentiles and the people of Israel in this city to conspire against your holy servant Jesus, whom you anointed. They did what your power and will had decided beforehand should happen. Now, Lord, consider their threats and enable your servants to speak your word with great boldness. Stretch out your hand to heal and perform miraculous signs and wonders through the Name of your holy servant Jesus. (Acts 4:24-30)

They used the Scriptures heavily in this prayer. Notice at least four places:

• *The reference to creation.* Besides the obvious reference to Genesis 1 and 2, they also had in mind Psalm 146:6, which goes like this: 'The Maker of Heaven and earth, the sea, and everything in them." They really believed that the Lord created all things. That encouraged them, because the One who made all things can certainly control all things. Have you explored the passages in the Bible that teach about God the Creator? Did you know that they can cause you to take hope in God for your daily problems, even serious problems like these men had?

• *The direct quote from Psalm 2.* They quoted from Psalm 2, the first two verses, word for word. You can follow their thinking very easily: the Maker of the world and everyone in it has not only the *ability* to rule the world, he has the *right* to rule over it. The disciples are going to the right person with their request to overrule the anti-Christian activities of their oppressors.

• *The prophecies of Christ's life and ministry.* They make reference to "what your power and will had decided beforehand should happen." Was it just a guess of theirs that God had decided beforehand what would happen to Christ? No — Jesus reminded them what his life would have to be like, over and over; and after his resurrection he explained it all again so that they would know that God had planned it all along. What did he use to explain it to them? "And beginning with *Moses and all the Prophets*, he explained to them what was said *in all the Scriptures* concerning himself." (Luke 24:27) They were thoroughly versed in what the Bible (Old Testament) said about Christ's life and ministry.

•   *The promise of the Spirit's ministry in the Church.* After quoting the passages from Psalms, you would think that they would interpret all that in just one way: that God would come down in wrath and squash all the resistance. But they knew their Bibles too well; that's not what they asked for. They didn't ask for a superficial fulfillment of Psalms, but an eternal, *spiritual* answer — the promised work of the Holy Spirit. Joel 2:28-32 is the classic passage in this regard, and the disciples themselves quoted from this text when the Spirit was poured out at Pentecost as proof that God works now, in this Gospel age, through his Spirit when he moves to rule over men and nations.

As you can see, the disciples knew how to use their Bibles when they prayed. They didn't just quote certain verses to make their prayer sound "Biblical" either; they had a deep understanding from studying it — they found meat for prayer in verses that perhaps you and I don't understand right away. They also put ideas together from different parts of the Bible, because they knew the Bible is its own best interpreter. One passage will give the correct meaning for another passage; we ought to be careful about jumping to conclusions about one text's meaning until we have studied what other texts have to say about it. After going through all this involved study, they felt that they could pray "in truth."

SUGGESTED PRACTICE

Praying with the Bible in hand may be a new experience to you. Don't feel that it's hopeless just because you don't know how to go about it. For one thing, you *must* learn how — so you can't give up now. Second, you aren't on your own; if you sincerely seek God his way, he will be found by you. The Spirit is in you because he is concerned that you get this right; he will not leave you alone to struggle on your own. (Romans 8:26-27)

First, *study* the Bible. You obviously can't pray according to his Word if you don't know anything about it. Spend a lot of time reading it. Think about what you are reading. When something grabs your interest, spend some time on just that passage; pull out some Bible study aids and dig in. If you aren't getting anything out of what you are reading, ask the Spirit to open the floodlights of Heaven on the text and show you the meaning. "If any of you lacks wisdom, he should ask God, who gives generously to all without finding fault, and it will be given to him." (James 1:5)

The more familiar you get with the Bible, the better chance you stand of praying in a way that pleases God. You may be an expert in some other field, or perhaps you aren't an expert in anything; but a Christian is called to be an expert in the Word of God. You *can* become well acquainted with the Bible. If you are a believer, it's not only possible to know a lot about the Bible, you *will* know a lot about it if you will only take the time to read and study it. It's not beyond the reach of the youngest Christian — the Spirit makes it plain for us to understand. There is no excuse for not knowing the Bible.

Second, pray on the spot, as you are reading. There are going to be things that you don't understand — ask God right there to reveal its meaning to you. He is faithful and he will help you to understand if you are really interested. It may take a little digging on your part, and some waiting on the Lord, but he honors those who wait on him by answering their prayers — even prayers about learning the Bible.

There are going to be things that move you as you read. God designed it to move you; after all, you are "born again" and now the things of God excite you and motivate you. Before you were alive to God you used to hear or read about God and his kingdom and walk away completely unimpressed; now, you should be willing to give your whole life for his cause and do anything he wants from you. You hate sin and love righteousness; you love your brothers and sisters in the Church; you hate the enemy; you long for truth and justice. There are new emotions and motivations in your heart that the Bible is designed to stir up and guide you in. If you can read God's Word and not pray then you aren't reading it well!

There are going to be things that bother you as you read. The Bible has a barbed tip that pierces the heart of sin; if you don't feel the pain when you read then you are holding yourself at arm's length from it. The Lord wants to talk to you about *you*, primarily; his aim is to save you, and the knife of the surgeon is going to hurt. But let it hurt! Who wouldn't want to be healed of a dreaded disease? And who of God's children would turn away from their Father's discipline if they see that his rod is a faithful "teacher of righteousness" that is designed to give life? As you read, lay yourself in front of him in humility and pray for the grace to receive his discipline.

Third, don't wander off to new texts until you get somewhere with the one you are studying. If there is one single reason that people don't get much out of Bible study, it's because they quit too soon. You probably won't get the full meaning of the text from your first or second reading; you would be surprised at how much material can be found in a small passage, if you spend the time at it. God's Word is like a never-ending stream of truth; wherever you dig, the truth just keeps welling up out of that spot like a spring of fresh water. Get ready to have a great deal to pray about from that one passage — that is, if the Spirit of God is truly involved in your study.

START WITH GOD'S NAME

Until now you have not asked for anything in my Name. Ask and you will receive, and your joy will be complete. (John 16:24)

Ever since we were little children we were taught to pray with these words at the end of our prayers: "In Jesus' name, Amen." It's an instinctive reaction. In fact, we wouldn't dare to pray without saying it! Not only would we have the feeling that God won't answer our prayers if we leave it out, somehow it makes us feel better if it is there at the end, dangling like a caboose on a train, closing up the prayer the way God likes to see it. It adds a necessary ceremonial touch.

The problem about ceremony is that sometimes it can be more superstition than reality. "Superstition" means doing something simply because you are afraid not to. There's no particular reason why someone does it, and if put to the test a person may not even *know* why he does it. But he can't bring himself to quit because he is afraid that something bad would happen, or at least that nothing good would happen, if he stopped doing this thing.

Most people feel the same way about the phrase "In Jesus' Name, Amen." The only reason they say it is because of the Lord's command in John 16:24; they are afraid not to say it because something bad might happen. Or at least they think that God will only hear their prayers if they are careful to include it at the end. The result is that they are saying words that really don't mean anything beyond giving them a warm feeling that everything is all right that ends right.

Jesus definitely told us to pray in his Name; there's no question about that. The question is, what exactly did he mean by that? Did he mean for us to use this formula at the end of our prayers? Does that accomplish what he intended? Is his name no more than a superstition, an empty ceremony? Or does that formula open the doors of Heaven and bring down answers? Or did he mean something far different than what we understand this verse in John to mean?

We can be sure that the disciples understood Jesus perfectly, especially after the Spirit was poured out on the Church. When they prayed, they followed the Lord's instructions on prayer that he gave here in John and on other occasions. Yet when we study their prayers, one obvious fact stands out like a sore thumb: none of them ended their prayers with "In Jesus' name, Amen." *None* of them. And yet they certainly took the Lord's counsel seriously! They were always careful to pray in Jesus' Name.

If it isn't obvious to us that the disciples really did pray in his Name, it's because we don't understand what the Lord was referring to. We need to find out more about the significance of the Lord's Name and how it affects our prayers.

NAMES MEAN SOMETHING

Everything has a name, and there is one basic reason for that: so that we can identify it. Instead of trying to identify the object that we mean by pointing at it, we invent a name that represents that object; with that name we can hold a conversation with others without always pointing here and there. Everyone is agreed on what an object's name will be so that there won't be any confusion about it.

Those names aren't just any sound that popped into someone's head, however. Hopefully we will pick a name that describes that object. In other words, the name-word itself has a meaning of its own, and someone attaches that word to the object they wish to name. For instance, the word "glass" refers to a clear, hard, brittle substance that man forms into many objects. From that word we have named other objects — for example, "glasses" that people wear on their noses in order to see; a "glass" for drinking from; a "looking glass" or mirror; and so on. Notice that the basic ideas of glass — clear, hard and brittle — are applied to each object by naming them "glass."

People in Bible times used names to describe their world just like we do. They named their children with words that meant something, though those names didn't necessarily describe their children any more than our names describe us. We name our children 'Irma" (noble); "Lloyd" (gray-haired); "Carol" (strong, womanly); though they may not turn out quite like that! People in the Old Testament named their children "Azriel" (help of God); "Zebul" (to dwell); "Helah" (rust). Often they picked names that sounded nice, or names that had been in the family for centuries, or names that were currently popular.

At any rate, a name served to identify someone or something; it separated that object from everything else and made it unique. Sometimes a person's name reflected a characteristic of that person, and almost always an object's name gave a person an idea of what that object was like.

THE NAME OF GOD

In God's case the concept of "name" takes on a profound dimension. His Name means so much to him that the Scripture tells us he is actually jealous for his Name's sake:

> But I have raised you up for this very purpose, that I might show you my power and that my Name might be proclaimed in all the earth. (Exodus 9:16)

> "Because he loves me," says the LORD, "I will rescue him; I will protect him, for he acknowledges my Name." (Psalm 91:14)

> I am the LORD; that is my Name! I will not give my glory to another or my praise to idols. (Isaiah 42:8)

> My covenant was with him, a covenant of life and peace, and I gave them to him; this called for reverence and he revered me and stood in awe of my Name. (Malachi 2:5)

But the Lord said to Ananias, "Go! This man is my chosen instrument to carry my Name before the Gentiles and their kings and before the people of Israel." (Acts 9:15)

I know your deeds. See, I have placed before you an open door that no one can shut. I know that you have little strength, yet you have kept my Word and have not denied my Name. (Revelation 3:8)

He is so concerned that people use his Name rightly that he made his Name the topic of one of his greatest commandments:

You shall not misuse the Name of the LORD your God, for the LORD will not hold anyone guiltless who misuses his Name. (Exodus 20:7)

That in itself should alert us to the supreme importance of God's Name. What is it about God's Name that makes it so special? Why is God so concerned to preserve its honor? What should we know about God's Name?

- *He has many names.* There is so much that is important to know about God that we need many names in order to understand him. His names fill both Old and New Testaments, and they all describe a different facet of his character and work. Our job is to find those names and use them to get a good grasp on who God is.

  There are two main groups of names for God: the names that *he* told us about, and the names that men made to describe what *they* discovered about him when they dealt with him. In both cases it's a revelation when we learn his Name; unless God tells us his Name we would never know it, and when we come close to him we find that he can be described in a particular way by this particular Name — which we never knew about him before we saw him.

Another way that we can divide his names is into these two groups: names that describe his *character*, and names that describe his *work*.

Here are some of the names of God:

LORD — This is the most important name of God in the Old Testament. Notice that the letters are in all caps; some versions, instead of translating the Hebrew word (which, by the way, is יהוה, or YHWH), render it "Yahweh" or "Jehovah." The Lord explained what the name means to Moses in Exodus 34:6-7 –

> *The LORD, the LORD, the compassionate and gracious God, slow to anger, abounding in love and faithfulness, maintaining love to thousands, and forgiving wickedness, rebellion and sin. Yet he does not leave the guilty unpunished; he punishes the children and their children for the sin of the fathers to the third and fourth generation.*

Lord — This name, in small letters, is the translation of the Hebrew "Adonai" — which means "master" and was the common title that underlings used of any superior being, be he man or god.

God Almighty — The Hebrew words are "El Shaddai" and it means more than you would think. "Shaddai" has its roots in the word for "breast" — which points to the idea of nourishment, resources, taking care of needs. The name could be better translated this way: "The God who has all necessary resources at hand for taking care of his children."

LORD of Hosts — This refers to the vast armies of angels that travel with him when he has work to do on the earth. Not that he needs any of them, but it makes an impressive sight to see so many willing servants under one banner.

The Rock — David calls him this because he found God to be an unshakable place to stand when everything around him was in turmoil.

The Redeemer — The custom in the Old Testament, when someone died and had no children to inherit his estate, was for the closest of kin to claim or "redeem" the estate (along with the widow) in order to carry on the man's name. The book of Ruth describes the process of redemption. God is a Redeemer when he claims us from death and gives us his family name.

The God of Abraham, Isaac, and Jacob — The reason he calls himself this is because he is the *same* God that the patriarchs knew. He dealt with them in a particular way, and he continues to deal with people now in the same way. The covenant he made with them is the same covenant he has with all his children. They are our spiritual forefathers; if we want God, we have to have *their* God.

The Fear of Isaac — This is a fascinating name in that it only appears in one place in the entire Bible — Genesis 31:42 & 53. I wonder if it refers to the fact that it was this God who once demanded Isaac's death as a sacrifice -and Isaac never forgot that!

God the Father — A name that we are more familiar with. It reflects some awesome realities, however: he is the Father of Christ his only Son; he is our Father in that he adopted us as his children; he has an inheritance waiting for us, the riches of his treasures in Heaven; he treats us as sons — royal treatment, sometimes discipline, but always as a loving Father working for the best of his children.

———

Jesus himself has a remarkable number of names, again in both the Old and the New Testaments. You would think that his story would be limited to the New

Testament; but the Old Testament not only predicted his coming and his ministry, it had a great deal to teach us about him. We have to learn about Christ from the Old Testament too if we want to fully understand him! There are things in the Old Testament — for instance, what his names are — that the New doesn't bother to go over again; therefore if we turn a deaf ear to the Old we will have gaping holes in our understanding of the Lord's person and work.

Here are some of the many names that Christ has:

Messiah — This is actually a Hebrew word; the Greek translation is "Christ." The meaning of both is "the anointed one" — referring first of all to pouring oil on one's head in a ceremonial ritual that showed authority. In a deeper sense, however, Jesus was anointed with the Holy Spirit (that was what the oil actually symbolized in his case) which gives him the power and authority of God to do his work here on earth.

Cornerstone — Peter considers Jesus Christ to be the stone that keeps the entire Church in line. (1 Peter 2:6) People use a cornerstone to fix one end of the building, and to identify the building in some way by engraving its name on it.

Foundation — Paul calls Christ the foundation of the Church. (1 Corinthians 3:11) The Lord holds all of us up from sinking into sin and death; if it weren't for his constant work in that regard, we would never be saved. Christian ministers have to keep that in mind — they have to build the believers' lives on the person and work of Christ or they will accomplish nothing. Otherwise they will watch their people sink under their sins and burdens.

Bread — In John 6 Jesus offended his hearers when he called himself "bread from Heaven." But it's true; Christians find in him spiritual nourishment when they are starving on the empty husks that this world is filled with.

Vine — Jesus said he is the vine to which we are all connected; like branches on a tree, we get all our supplies from him. (John 15:1-17) He is a never-ending source of spiritual necessities. If the vine is good, and if we are connected to him, we will bear appropriate fruit.

The Lord Our Righteousness — In Jeremiah 23:6 we have a prediction of the special work of Christ, the reason that the people of God need him so badly: *he himself* will be our righteousness by satisfying the Law completely in our place.

King of kings — (Revelation 17:14) Men don't rule themselves; the Lord Jesus has the hearts of kings in his hand. He rules over everyone even if they have no awareness of his rule over them; and he accomplishes his will in this world even in the face of all the opposition of men.

The Way — If someone wants to get to God, there is only one way — through Christ. (John 14:6) We have to listen to him, we have to follow him, we have to trust him for certain things, and we have to do his will. Only if we follow all these steps will we find God. Nobody else and nothing else will get us there.

The Head of the Church — He has the preeminent position over all of us who make up the Church. (Ephesians 1:10) He decides what is to be done, as the head of the body leads the whole body.

———

God the Spirit also has names that reflect what he does for us:

The Holy Spirit — If you would see God face to face, the single thing about him that would strike you the most is his holiness. That's what Isaiah saw and heard when he came before the throne of God. "Holy, holy, holy is the LORD Almighty; the whole earth is full of his glory." (Isaiah 6:3) And when God calls someone and makes that person into a child of God, he sends his Spirit into them — so that they will live in the presence of his holiness at all times, day and night, in whatever they do. That means that *they* are going to be holy too!

The Spirit of truth — God the Spirit is always working to get the truth into us. That's one of his primary jobs, mainly because we are so ignorant and in need of truth. We live in a world full of darkness and lies, and we have been trained in the world's lies since we were born. We have much to learn about God! If we are going to learn anything about God and be saved from sin and death, the Spirit must reveal new things to us that we never knew before, information that we won't get anywhere else. He doesn't come up with absolutely new information, however; he teaches us the words of God. "When the Counselor comes, whom I will send to you from the Father, the Spirit of truth who goes out from the Father, he will testify about me." (John 15:26) He opens our eyes so that we can see the realities of Heaven, and see this world in the light from Heaven. We can walk by faith because of what the Spirit helps us see.

The Comforter — The Spirit also comforts those who need a soothing touch to their hearts. It's a difficult thing to grow a tender flower in a howling desert. It's also not easy for a new-born Christian to live in a hostile world, surrounded by enemies (who may even be those of his own household!), called to do impossible tasks, hoping for a reward that he can't see. So the Spirit provides much-needed comfort in the face of this adversity, encouraging the believer that he isn't working *for no reason* and that the promises of God are certain in Christ. (2 Corinthians 1:20)

These names of God — the Father, Son, and Spirit — are only a small sample of the names given in the Bible. One could spend a lifetime studying them all. At the very least we should take some time studying some of these names and learning exactly what they mean, and why they are so appropriately given to God.

- *His Name distinguishes him from other gods.* During the time of the Israelites there were scores of gods filling the heavens, according to the beliefs of the pagan nations around them. Each tribe worshipped its own version of some god or another. And unfortunately these gods shared a lot of names that our God has — because it is easy for us to attach whatever name we like to a god, even if it isn't true.

The difference is that only the God of the Bible really fits the description in the name. A false god may claim to be a savior, but if he doesn't save then where is his credibility? A pagan worshiper may call his god a refuge, but where is that god when trouble comes?

We today have the same problem. There are a lot of things in our world that claim to give us peace, to give us wisdom, to give us strength — but do they make good on their claims? Isn't it rather the case that our modern god also turns out to be a failure in the end? The god is a cheat and a lie, and we didn't get from it what we were hoping for. Non-Christian religions are suffering under the same deceit — their description of God turns out to be a hoax, because it doesn't address the deepest needs in a human soul for the true God, and it doesn't describe the true God as he works in this world.

But the God of Israel is true to his names. When we find him and talk to him, we discover that he *really is* what his Name says he is. Nobody else can claim to be like him in any way; that's what his glory is all about.

For instance, when someone came to Jesus and called him "good teacher," he objected to the title, as if anybody is good apart from God — "'Why do you call me good?' Jesus answered. 'No one is good — except God alone.' " (Mark 10:18) His names show us the highest, purest, most unchangeable, most glorious example of what the Name describes; everything and everyone else is either a poor copy of him or the opposite of him.

You will find genuine help when you turn to him for what his Name teaches. He isn't the disappointment that other "helps" turn out to be; he proves to be "able to do immeasurably more than all we ask or imagine." (Ephesians 3:20)

You are aware that some doctors give their more exasperating patients sugar pills — pills that don't have any medicinal value — because their ailments are all in their heads. They are happy enough thinking that the medicine is doing them wonders when it isn't doing a thing in the world for them. But doctors give the real stuff to someone who is genuinely sick. In the same way, all the pleasures and powers and knowledge that are in this world are of no more value to a human soul than sugar pills; their names mean nothing; they are making empty claims. But when God helps someone and gives them wisdom and strengthens them in their weakness, that person comes away changed. It's like the time when Moses saw God on Mt. Sinai: he came away from the encounter glowing with a strange light around his head. (Exodus 34:29-35) No other power on earth can impact us like that. Moses was *changed* after his encounter with Yahweh.

God's success rate is phenomenal. No other candidate for our worship can show such a perfect record of being what he promised he would be. David said that "I have never seen the righteous forsaken or their children begging bread." (Psalm 37:25) Paul was so confident in God, after a lifetime of finding him utterly dependable and true to his great Name, that he could say in the face of physical persecution that "I know whom I have believed, and am convinced that he is able to guard what I have entrusted to him for that day." (2 Timothy 1:12) When Paul needed a refuge, the Lord gathered Paul under his protective hands. When Paul needed wisdom, the Lord filled his mouth with words from Heaven. Paul could testify to the truth of the Lord's many names from first hand experience.

This is the meaning of glory. When God gets the credit for being what he claims he is, that glorifies him. When someone else claims that credit for themselves then he is dishonored. That's why he is so jealous about his Name — he wants everyone to know that *only he* is the Refuge, *only he* is the Savior, *only he* is the Bread from Heaven, *only he* is the Shepherd. If anybody else takes these names on themselves then people will think that God isn't what they need after all — that they need more than God! He will never settle for that.

• *His Name is a handle for prayer.* Finding God has always been the most difficult job of any religion. Many religions simply don't try; they are content to talk *about* God (or the god of their own making, at any rate), and they hope that nobody asks them to come up with a real God. Other religions at least try to find some supernatural force that is higher than man, but unfortunately they either fail, or find an evil spirit who masquerades as a god.

But Old Testament Judaism and New Testament Christianity have made good on their claim of actually getting in touch with the real God. One reason is because God has come close to us, in visions and through the work of angels and especially in the Lord Jesus Christ. But another reason that we can claim to have actually come into God's presence is that our prayers open the doors of Heaven, allowing us to walk inside.

God's names serve as handles to the gates of his kingdom. What a blessing that God has given us a handle to the mysteries of his spiritual world! When we grasp that handle then the door swings wide open and we *see* this God that we are after. There are many people in the world who pray night and day, without ceasing, and don't ever see God. It's all wasted effort and they may as well quit. They are trying to open Heaven's doors by prying at the edges with their fingernails instead of grasping the handle of God's Name. But a Christian will find the Lord's Name, get a good hold on that, and end up in God's presence as a result.

Did you ever try to pick up a barrel of water without handles? You couldn't hope to move it, it's so heavy and awkward; even if someone helps you, it won't budge. But put handles on it and you can easily move it to wherever you want. Well, the business of prayer is a job that the best of us can't manage, because it deals with eternity, with judgment, with struggling against dark powers in the air, with spiritual realities that we can't see. Our very lives hang in the balance. This is too much for anybody to tackle without some handles to get hold of it properly. In his mercy God has provided a way that we can accomplish real work when we pray; we can actually get somewhere in our struggle against sin and in our growth in grace — by using his names as handles to carry our faith to him and his grace back into our hearts.

One more analogy. A car becomes a deadly weapon when the steering system quits. But if we can steer it properly then the car takes us where we want to go. If you use God's names as steering mechanisms for your prayer then you will pray in such a way as to achieve your goal — you will get where you want to go in your prayer. Without his names, you will run wide of the mark of true prayer; you will be out in the field somewhere, bouncing around in confusion, not knowing what to ask for or how to receive anything from God, and you certainly won't end up with answers from him. But his names tell you what to pray *for*, and *how* to pray for it, and give you encouragement that you are headed in the right direction. There's nothing like a good firm grip on the steering wheel for assurance that things are OK; there's nothing like taking hold of God's Name when you pray to assure you that you are on the right track, that you will get his attention and his answers.

• *We are to call on his Name.* The purpose of someone having a name is so that we can call them and get their attention. Of course, you have to use the right name for the right person; if you would yell "Bill!" when you really wanted Bob, Bob isn't going to turn around (maybe some non-Bills will turn around but only out of curiosity; they know that you don't want them.) And if you don't even call them, no matter what their name, then you won't get their attention at all.

This brings us to one of the most tragic aspects of Jewish history. The special name of God in the Old Testament — YHWH, or as we put it, the LORD — was unique to the God of the Israelites. This was the Name that he gave them to use when they worshipped him; this name distinguished him from other gods. He even poured tremendously important meaning into that Name (see Exodus 34:6-7). But over the centuries, because of an overly zealous respect for the holiness of God's special Name, the Jews made up rules about it. First, nobody was allowed to speak that Name; it was too holy for a sinner to even pronounce and make dirty with his sinful lips. Second, whenever the rabbi was reading in the Bible and he came to this holy Name, he was not to pronounce it even then — he was to say "Adonai" instead and go on around it. Third, the scribes, when they wrote their books of interpretation of the Biblical text, weren't even supposed to write the holy Name. The only way they could represent it was to write the first and last letters only, like this: Y"H. Furthermore, the problem was compounded by the fact that Hebrew didn't have any vowels — for *any* word, let alone the holy Name. So all they had were the consonants: YHWH.

The result was that, over time, everyone forgot how to pronounce God's special Name! Nobody, not even the scholars, could remember what the vowels were supposed to be. In their fanatical zeal to preserve the holiness of his Name they ended up with a Name they couldn't even use!

What makes this even more tragic is that this was the Name that God *told them to call on* if they wanted to be saved! "Everyone who calls on the Name of the LORD will be saved." (Joel 2:32) If they refused to even pronounce it, how could they hope to be saved?

We Christians aren't superstitious about his Name like the Jews were. But we have our own problems about his Name: we don't even think about using it. We think there's no power or benefit in using it. So we also don't call on the Name of the Lord. That's what Jesus was referring to when he accused his disciples: "Until now you have not asked for anything in my Name." We have these vast resources at our disposal, these handles to the door of Heaven, and we don't use them. We leave behind the very things that he told us will get his attention and his interest.

"The LORD will hear when I call to him." (Psalm 4:3) There's the promise. But there's the responsibility too: if you address him by Name then you can expect to get somewhere with the Lord. Otherwise, forget it.

• *He responds to his Name.* Just like anybody who turns around to face us when we call their name, the

Lord will do the same with us when we call him by his special names. He knows that he is the *only* one we could be referring to! Nobody else can rightfully claim the full meaning of that Name.

There are many Scriptures that quote God's promise to us that he will answer when we call on him. But probably the most powerful example of how he responds to his Name is found in the story of the Temple that Solomon built. Read the story once and you may miss the significance of what God is saying about this temple; read it a few more times and this idea of his Name starts becoming more obvious:

> I have chosen and consecrated this Temple so that my Name may be there forever. My eyes and my heart will always be there. (2 Chronicles 7:16)

Solomon understood from the very beginning that this was to be the place where God's Name would be:

> But will God really dwell on earth with men? The Heavens even the highest Heavens, cannot contain you. How much less this Temple I have built! . . . May your eyes be open toward this Temple day and night, this place of which you said you would put your Name there. May you hear the prayer your servant prays toward this place. (2 Chronicles 6:18,20)

In other words, his Name has a place near us — where we can take hold of it, call on him with it in prayer, and be assured that he will "hear from Heaven, your dwelling place." (2 Chronicles 6:21) God had the Temple built just for this purpose!

Look at his next Temple — Jesus; the same principle is in operation there:

I have revealed your Name[1] to those whom you gave me out of the world . . . Holy Father, protect them by the power of your Name — the Name you gave me — so that they may be one as we are one. (John 17:6,11)

The One through whom we may be saved has come close to us, "closer than a brother," close enough to touch him and hear him, so that we can call on him and be saved. "The Word is near you; it is in your mouth and in your heart." (Romans 10:8) This proves God's intention to answer when we call his Name.

PRAYING IN HIS NAME

It should be pretty obvious by now that God's many names are extremely important for prayer. We can't expect to get anywhere without using them in some way. Furthermore, the Lord himself promised that he will respond to his names if we will just begin using them; in fact, he *commands* us to use his Name — he threatens that he *won't answer us* if we leave his Name out of our prayers.

We need to look again at how to use God's Name in prayer, this time from a more practical standpoint.

- *Find a name that fits your needs* — The Lord has specific names that he will respond to, names that glorify him and hold him up as the only God. And you have specific needs — that's why you are praying in the first place. So study his names to see if your needs and his names match up.

---

[1] It's unfortunate that the NIV Bible didn't translate what the Greek original says here. The word "name" is in the original text, but the translators didn't see the importance attached to God's Name in this context. But when we consider the tremendous importance attached to God's Name elsewhere in Scripture, and how Jesus refers several times to God's Name in this very prayer, then we must insist that the English translation include the word.

Philip Henry, a preacher of the seventeenth century and father of the famous Bible commentator Matthew Henry, preached a series of sermons once on the names of Christ. It is a rich feast to read the sermon notes. He laid out 54 names of the Lord in his sermons; here they are:

Foundation, Food, Root, Clothing, Head, Hope, Refuge, Righteousness, Light, Life, Peace, Passover, Portion, Propitiation, Freedom, Fountain, Wisdom, Way, Banner, Example, Door, Dew, Sun, Shield, Strength, Song, Horn, Honor, Sanctification, Supply, Resurrection, Redemption, Lesson, Ladder, Truth, Treasure, Temple, Ark, Altar, Our All, Husband, Father, Brother, Friend, Master, Teacher, King, Captain, Physician, Advocate, Shepherd, Elder, Inhabitant, Keeper.

Do you see anything in this list that you need for your life? I should hope so! God thinks that you need these things; that's why he sent Jesus to be these things for you. Consider them a spiritual smorgasbord: as you read the Bible, you can see the rich foods on God's table, all labeled by name. Your hunger will drive you to this food and that food to satisfy you, and the Father stands ready like a chef to serve you whatever you want.

• *Beginning, middle, and ending* — By all means use God's Name *all through* your prayer, not just at the end. Even if you begin your prayer with his Name, don't quit there — continue using it and revolving around it all through your prayer until you wind up.

This means, of course, that you must understand what his Name means. Most people don't know enough about his Name to make a whole prayer about it; but that's not an excuse — that's the point! God's Name *describes* him; if we don't know enough about God to focus in on him during a prayer, then it's about time we spent some solid hours studying the Bible and learning who our God really is.

His names should give us ideas for prayer. They contain a lot of data about God, and if we really know who God is then we should be able to find things to talk to him about. For example, if we know just how holy he is then that means several things:

He is called "Holy, Holy, Holy" — (Isaiah 6:3) — it is no game to come to God in prayer; he demands that everyone who comes to him be holy just as he is holy. He hates to look at sin. If we have sin to take care of, then we shouldn't be surprised when he brings it up during prayer. If we are hiding something in our hearts, then he isn't going to listen to us. If we have sinned against our brother then he is going to demand that we take care of that matter before we come to him. There is this and much more involved in his name of "Holy, Holy, Holy."

He is called "The Holy One of Israel" — (Isaiah 48:17) — Not only is he holy himself, he intends to do whatever is necessary to make his people holy. Through the covenant he promised to deliver them from sin, to collect them together as a people called by his Name, to make a nation out of them, to give them his spiritual inheritance. Other nations can only look on with envy while God cares for his people with infinite love. He has given his Law only to his people; only to them has he given his Spirit who sanctifies the heart; only to them has he given the promise to live with them. The "Holy One of Israel" intends to make us holy so that we can live with him forever in Heaven.

His names should give us encouragement to pray. If we really understand his Name, that will motivate us to come to him about what that Name means. Someone who prays without much interest will wander during prayer; he won't be able to keep to the subject because prayer is just a dull ceremony that he feels he has to perform. But remember the widow who was determined to get justice from the judge? She banged on his door all night until he got up and gave her justice! She wasn't going to quit until he did what he had the power to do for her. And how did she know to go to him for this need? Because of his name: the judge. (Luke 18:1-8) Jesus pointed out in this story that this is the way you need to approach God — and his Name is going to motivate you to keep trying. If Jesus really is the "door" to Heaven, then of course you won't quit praying until you find yourself inside. If God really is the "God of Abraham, Isaac, and Jacob" then you will want God's covenant blessings that those men first received from him. If Jesus really is the "Shepherd" then you will want him to "lead you beside quiet waters" and restore your soul.

• *What did Jesus mean?* — When Jesus told his disciples that "until now you have not asked for anything in my Name," he was putting his finger on why they weren't getting answers from God when they prayed. "Ask and you will receive," he told them. What did he mean by this? Did he mean that they should tell God "You *must* answer my prayer — Jesus sent me!" I don't think that God is any more impressed with name-dropping than we are; he can tell when we don't know enough about the Lord to pray in faith and knowledge. Remember the sons of Sceva? They thought that it was enough to throw around Jesus' Name in order to get spiritual results — and they found out that they needed the *reality* of the Name too!

> Some Jews who went around driving out evil spirits tried to invoke the Name of the Lord Jesus over those who were demon-possessed. They would say, "In the Name of Jesus, whom Paul preaches, I command you to come out." Seven sons of Sceva, a Jewish chief priest, were doing

this. One day, the evil spirit answered them, "Jesus I know and I know about Paul, but who are you?" Then the man who had the evil spirit jumped on them and overpowered them all. He gave them such a beating that they ran out of the house naked and bleeding. (Acts 19:13-16)

Is this the way we use Jesus' Name when we pray? 1 don't know that God will "give us a beating" if we do, but we shouldn't expect any answers from him except perhaps an angry one! He feels that we must honor his Son's Name more than just using it as a ceremonial add-on to our prayers. After all, he sent Jesus to us specifically so that we would have the necessary means of coming to the Father in the right way.

What is that right way? It is to ask the Father for what he has given us in Christ. It is to see clearly what Jesus is to us — to understand his work that he did for our sake. It is to take hold of what God has sent down to us from Heaven. He gives, and we take and believe. That's what the Father wants to hear from us when we pray. He wants to see us focusing on Jesus, the treasure from Heaven that he is giving us. To pray in Christ's Name, then, is nothing less than to ask God for what Jesus is: "Father, give me the Shepherd for my soul; give me Light from Heaven so that I know how to walk in this dark world; give me Bread from Heaven so that I won't starve on the husks of this world, bring me to the Ark of the Covenant so that I can come and bow down in worship and get forgiveness." The Father wants to hear these Names of his Son on our lips when we have things to ask of him.

Think of it this way: Jesus instructed us to pray for *what is in* his Name — for all the fullness and richness and power and variety of his many names.

• *What you can expect* — When you pray in God's Name, you can expect simply this: that the Father will give you what you ask for. He is pleased when you focus on his Name and on the names of the Lord Jesus; he sees that you understand who your God is and what he really does; he wants to reward your faith in him by giving you *himself,* which is what you are actually asking for.

Our greatest joy is God himself. "I will give them a heart to know me, that I am the Lord. They will be my people, and I will be their God, for they will return to me with all their heart." (Jeremiah 24:7) "I am your shield, your very great reward." (Genesis 15:1) It is his rich variety that fascinates us and offers us so much hope for succeeding over our daily trials. These names of his reflect the many, many things that we find in him; you can do no better in your Christian walk than to discover the meaning and reality of God's Names:

> I said to the LORD, "You are my Lord; apart from you I have no good thing" ... The sorrows of those will increase who run after other gods ... LORD, you have assigned me my portion and my cup; you have made my lot secure. The boundary lines have fallen for me in pleasant places; surely I have a delightful inheritance ... You have made known to me the path of life; you will fill me with joy in your presence, with eternal pleasures at your right hand. (Psalm 16)

You can expect to experience more of the presence and reality of God when you focus on his Name. If it's him that you want and ask for, he will certainly come to you and answer your prayers.

• *Glorify his Name* — You aren't done until you make it known to Heaven and earth how true his names are. Have you found him to be a shepherd, a light, a Savior? Have you received what his names promised? Then testify to that! Tell others who are struggling to find those blessings that they will only be found in the Lord. Explain to others, who want to know why your life is so blessed, that it was the Lord who blessed you according to the truth in his Name. Let everyone know that the false gods are lying, that they are stealing the glory that is due to the Lord alone.

There isn't a more convincing salesman than someone who uses the product himself. He can easily praise it when it makes his own life more enjoyable. In the same way, Christians have something to talk about when they pray for what God's Name describes and God answers them with that reality. You can't convince *them* that God isn't real! They have *seen* these good things, they have *tasted* the things of Heaven, they have *experienced* the thrill of meeting God face to face and hearing him speak and feeling his hand on their hearts. The God that the Bible describes is real to them. His names really do describe who he is. And they can offer evidence in their own lives that his names are powerful tools for getting answers from prayer.

AN EXAMPLE PRAYER

They called David the "sweet singer of Israel" but they should also call him the Church's most preeminent prayer warrior. He knew how to pray! And he knew that he had to get a hold of God's Name if he wanted answers to his prayers.

Sometimes, though, he prayed without asking for anything in particular. For example, in Psalm 145 he simply praised God without making any requests. This prayer is remarkable because it is a good example of how much David knew about the Lord. Here is the prayer in its entirety:

1 A psalm of praise. Of David. I will exalt you, my God the King; I will praise your Name for ever and ever. 2 Every day I will praise you and extol your Name for ever and ever. 3 Great is the LORD and most worthy

of praise; his greatness no one can fathom. 4 One generation will commend your works to another; they will tell of your mighty acts. 5 They will speak of the glorious splendor of your majesty, and I will meditate on your wonderful works. 6 They will tell of the power of your awesome works, and I will proclaim your great deeds. 7 They will celebrate your abundant goodness and joyfully sing of your righteousness. 8 The LORD is gracious and compassionate, slow to anger and rich in love. 9 The LORD is good to all; he has compassion on all he has made. 10. All you have made will praise you, O LORD; your saints will extol you. 11 They will tell of the glory of your kingdom and speak of your might, 12 so that all men may know of your mighty acts and the glorious splendor of your kingdom. 13 Your kingdom is an everlasting kingdom, and your dominion endures through all generations. The LORD is faithful to all his promises and loving toward all he has made. 14 The LORD upholds all those who fall and lifts up all who are bowed down. 15 The eyes of all look to you and you give them their food at the proper time. 16 You open your hand and satisfy the desires of every living thing. 17 The LORD is righteous in all his ways and loving toward all he has made. 18 The LORD is near to all who call on him, to all who call on him in truth. 19 He fulfills the desires of those who fear him; he hears their cry and saves them. 20 The LORD watches over all who love him, but all the wicked he will destroy. 21 My mouth will speak in praise of the LORD. Let every creature praise his holy Name for ever and ever. (Psalm 145)

This is a prayer of praise, so we don't find David necessarily taking advantage, right now, of the truths in God's Name. He simply wants to lay it out on the table for inspection. Notice how easily he does this! We get the impression that he knew so much about God that he could have gone on praising his Name for hours. Pay attention to these things about David's prayer:

- *He starts off by focusing on God's Name.* In verses 1-2 he announces his intentions for this prayer: to tell about the wonderful things in God's Name. A worthy subject for anybody to pray about. But there's a particular Name that he's interested in this time — "my God the King." Why he chose that Name to look at, we don't know; perhaps he wanted to remind himself that he was not the highest king looking over Israel — perhaps the nation was struggling and he was struggling and he needed encouragement that someone else was in control of things. Whatever the reason, he homed in on this Name at the very beginning. And he also studied how Yahweh

— the LORD — whom the Israelites trusted for their salvation, is also the King over the entire earth; notice how he interweaves the name LORD with the idea of God the King.

• *He examines all the facets of God's Name and prays about them.* From verses 3 to 20 he studies the Lord's name, "God the King," in all its great variety. He talks about God's "greatness"; he refers to God's "acts" which have an effect on the kingdom and which will be remembered for generations. "Abundant goodness" and "righteousness" are qualities that make him a king deserving of praise from his subjects; they are the receivers of all that goodness and righteousness. Then (verses 8-9) he looks at how gently and compassionately the Lord deals with his subjects; God could very well use his tremendous power to strike the world in wrath, but instead he has this quality about him that makes us love him.

In verse 13 David sees that God is no temporary king. The Lord will rule the universe forever; which means that the plans that God started out with, he will see through to the end. All other kings have to hand their hard work over to another when they die, and as Solomon observed, "who knows whether he will be a wise man or a fool?" (Ecclesiastes 2:19) But the Lord God will rule forever doing his will forever, seeing the fruit of his work, building things just like he wants to see it, ending up with an eternal Church.

In the rest of the prayer David studies how God takes care of his subjects and their personal needs. What other king can claim to have such a perfect record? What we all wish for in a leader, God truly is in a way that nobody else can dream of being.

• *He ends up with God's Name.* At the end of the prayer David returns to the Lord's Name (not by saying it again but by referring to it). He feels that he successfully got a grasp on what "God the King" means in this prayer, and he calls on others to see the same glory in God's Name and praise him for it.

Notice how David stuck to the Name all through the prayer. There was much to pray about in this Name; in fact, one could take any of these individual ideas behind the Name "God the King" and form a prayer around just that one element. His prayer is saturated with God's Name from beginning to end. He didn't wait until the end of the prayer before he even mentioned God's Name! Instead, he let it guide what he prayed about, which means he had to focus on that Name from the very start.

SUGGESTED PRACTICE

Praying according to God's Name may not be the easiest thing you've ever tried, especially if you aren't used to using his Name in prayer. But there are things that you can do in order to get more used to it.

- *Make lists of his names.* Make your own list of God's names — for the Father, the Son, and the Holy Spirit — taking them from both the Old and New Testaments. Don't limit your list to one of the three persons; the triune God has always worked in this world and among his people, so we can see all three of them in his work.

  When you make these lists, try to find the meaning of the name used. Some of God's names in the Old Testament may be Hebrew words, and you will need a Hebrew dictionary or some other help (Strong's Concordance has one in the back) to find out the meaning of the word. Other names are more evident (like "refuge") but don't assume that you know the meaning of even these names. Often what *we* mean by the word isn't what God is referring to; obviously you have to find out what God meant by it. The context (the particular place in Scripture surrounding where you find the Name) will often give you a clue to God's meaning for his Name; if not, find another passage in the Bible that may help.

- *Study why his name is appropriate for your prayer.* This requires application — taking the things of God and applying them to our lives. We aren't very good at this. We are usually content with admiring Scriptural truths and then forgetting them in the concerns of daily living. But remember, these names tell us things about God that we desperately need. He gave them to us, to be used when we need what that Name describes.

This means that you should study his Name well enough that you have a good idea of how to use it. Find out how the saints in the Bible used this Name. What did they appeal to in it? Why did it encourage them? Why do you need it?

• *Keep his Name in focus while you pray.* By all means keep in mind who you are talking to. Probably the toughest part of prayer is to keep your thoughts and attention on God instead of yourself and everything else; the mind tends to wander from the purpose too easily. But you can do this if you think about his Name all the way through the prayer. By this method you can more easily come back to the reason you are praying in the first place.

Don't misunderstand the point of this chapter: I'm not saying that you can't end your prayer with "In Jesus' Name, Amen." If you really want to do that then by all means do it; that is entirely between you and the Lord. The point is that you should have been praying in Jesus' Name *all the way through the prayer*, not just at the end as an afterthought. His Name should have been the guiding light that led you to the God that you know by Name. If you haven't really prayed in his Name, then no amount of piety will make that ending "In Jesus' Name, Amen" less obnoxious to God; he knows the thoughts and intents of your heart, and he knows if you have any idea of what you are talking about. "You shall not misuse the Name of the LORD your God, for the LORD will not hold anyone guiltless who misuses his Name." (Exodus 20:7) If you can see the real God when you pray then you are going to call him by his real Name.

PRAY IN THE SPIRIT

And pray in the Spirit on all occasions with all kinds of prayers and requests. (Ephesians 6:18)

In the last few decades the Holy Spirit has been at the forefront of discussion in the Church. Even churches and denominations that historically have had little to say about the work of the Spirit have had to deal with the new charismatic and Pentecostal movements that have swept through Christian circles everywhere. And this means, of course, that there are all sorts of theories on what the Holy Spirit actually does.

The argument about the Spirit's role in prayer is no less heated. There are many opinions on how much the Spirit is involved in our prayers, and what he does for us during prayer. Christians hold to positions all the way from "prayer languages" and ecstatic tongues to a warm, general feeling of oneness with other people in the worship service. Most people, no doubt, don't even know what the Spirit has to do with prayer and so they don't even think about it.

Probably the reason that so many people are confused about the issue is because the Spirit is, by definition, someone (some people would say "something") who works in our hearts, our seat of emotions; and it's too easy to confuse what we feel there with what the Spirit might be doing. And who's to say that someone's feelings are wrong? If he feels something very strongly, wouldn't he naturally attribute it to the Spirit's work and we simply have to accept his statement? Didn't Jesus say that the Spirit is like the wind, which "blows wherever it pleases"? (John 3:8) Who is to say what is of the Spirit and what isn't? How do we know that someone's feelings are not from God?

This confusion isn't necessary, however. We can know what is of the Spirit and what isn't by applying some simple tests. For one thing, the Spirit glorifies Christ whenever he works — he draws our attention to Christ in some way, so that we learn about him and learn to trust him in some way. (John 14:2) For another, the Spirit never works in a way that contradicts the Word of God.

But what about prayer? What does the Spirit have to do with prayer? Can we know if he is near us when we pray? Fortunately we don't have to analyze our feelings to see if we are being "spiritual enough", nor is it just a guess as to whether we are praying "in the Spirit." We can know. There is a clear explanation for this in the Scriptures. What we have to do is back up and look at the bigger picture — we have to study what the Spirit does generally in people's lives. When we find those general principles, it will be easier to see how he helps us pray.

Is it important to know how the Spirit helps us pray? Yes — this verse from Ephesians is a command, not wishful thinking. Paul tells them to pray in the Spirit "on all occasions" with "all kinds of prayers and requests," not just when they think about it. In the first place, it must be something that we can do. It must be pretty easy to tell when we pray "in the Spirit" because he tells us to make sure that we do. Second, he doesn't seem to allow other options. He wants us to pray "in the Spirit" every chance we get. It seems that prayers that aren't "in the Spirit" don't count with him; he evidently considers them so much wasted time.

If these two points are true, then it's time we understood something about praying "in the Spirit." We should find out if we have been doing it, and if we haven't then we need to learn how; we need to *start* doing it. But first let's look at what the special work of the Spirit is; that will give us a clue about how to pray in the Spirit.

THE WORK OF THE SPIRIT

The Holy Spirit has had just as much to do with man as God the Father and God the Son. You will find him working all through the Bible, Old and New Testaments. In fact, some passages that talk simply of God or the Lord often describe situations where it is obviously the Spirit who is really at work.

Usually we think of the Spirit in terms of sanctification — that is, making us free from sin, or holy. "But you were washed, you were sanctified, you were justified in the name of the Lord Jesus Christ and by the Spirit of our God." (1 Corinthians 6:11) "To God's elect ... who have been chosen according to the foreknowledge of God the Father, by the sanctifying work of the Spirit, for obedience to Jesus Christ and sprinkling by his blood." (1 Peter 1:1-2)

But that's not the *primary* work of the Spirit according to the Bible. In a total of over 80 different passages that talk about what the Spirit does, I found only five places where it refers to his work of cleansing from sin, and some of those are marginal. Over half of the passages teach that the Spirit *reveals* the things of God, and the other half talk about the Spirit's *revitalizing* work.

- *The Spirit reveals the world of God.* "'No eye has seen, no ear has heard, no mind has conceived what God has prepared for those who love him' — but God has revealed it to us by his Spirit." (1 Corinthians 2:9-10)

If we want to know more about Heaven, the first hurdle that we have to get over is the fact that we are so earthbound. Since the day we were born, we have known only what we can see, smell, touch, taste, and hear. This world that we live in has been, to us, the only real world, as far as we can tell. The things that we put value on and the things that we own are in this world; the issues that we consider important are in this world; the people we respect are in this world; the forces that we fear are in this world. Most people live and die knowing nothing more than what is in this physical world, and they really don't care if there is another world — it seems like unrealistic stories anyway, myths and fairy tales.

But there is another world that is different than this one, even if we don't know anything about it: it's the world that God lives in. God is not of this world. That is a fundamental doctrine of Christianity; we have to believe that God's world is a completely different place than this world that we live in, that he can and does exist without any dependence on the physical world. He is the Creator: he made the universe, and he doesn't depend on it in the least — it depends on him. We could all snap completely out of existence and he would not change in the least. He is what he is, and he will always be what he is, without our help or interference.

God's world is completely different than ours. Whereas ours is always changing, always deteriorating and building up, his is unchanging. Ours is completely physical, which means that the One who made it can unmake it just as easily as he made it (which he intends to do someday, by the way); but God's world is spiritual and therefore eternal. Our world looks good on the outside, and promises to satisfy us — but they are hollow promises because it can't deliver on those promises (God intentionally made it unable to satisfy us); God's world doesn't look so appealing to our senses but it does satisfy the soul's deepest needs. Our world struggles under the curse of sin and death, and God has already passed judgment on it — its time will come; God's world remains untouched by that stain and therefore remains God's only choice for where spiritual life can be had.

Now here is this completely "other" world that we don't know anything about; we can, and do, live our entire lives in complete ignorance that it even exists. The two worlds actually run parallel to each other, like two cities on either side of a railroad track; and if it weren't for certain historical events that forced a link between the two we would still not know how the people lived "on the other side of the tracks."

One of the most important historical events that forged a bridge between the two worlds was the giving of the Holy Spirit. The Spirit reveals, makes plain, uncovers, makes "see-able" this other world that God lives in. It's like taking the veil away from a statue so that the public can see it for the first time. It is like opening a window into Heaven so that we can see inside.

The first occasion in the Bible where we find the Spirit doing this type of work is in connection with the Tabernacle. God was concerned that Moses and the Israelites build their central place of worship in the right way; not just anything would do. So instead of running the risk that the makers of the Tabernacle would misunderstand his instructions, no matter how plain he made them, the Lord poured out his Spirit on the two men in charge of the building project:

> See, the LORD has chosen Bezalel son of Uri, the son of Hur, of the tribe of Judah, and he has filled him with the Spirit of God, with skill, ability and knowledge in all kinds of crafts ... And he has given both him and Oholiab son of Ahisamach, of the tribe of Dan, the ability to teach others . . . so Bezalel, Oholiab and every skilled person to whom the LORD has given skill and ability to know how to carry out all the work of constructing the sanctuary are to do the work just as the LORD has commanded. (Exodus 35:30,34-35; 36:1)

And what did the Spirit show them?

> They serve at a sanctuary that is a copy and shadow of what is in Heaven. This is why Moses was warned when he was about to build the tabernacle: "See to it that you make

everything according to the pattern shown you on the mountain." (Hebrews 8:5)

The Spirit showed these men what the Heavenly Tabernacle, in God's world, looked like; to what extent we don't know, but at least we know that they saw the essentials so that they could pattern the earthly tabernacle after it in a way that would satisfy God.

In Isaiah there is a prophecy of the Messiah, and it tells us that he will have the Spirit:

> The Spirit of the LORD will rest upon him — the Spirit of wisdom and of understanding, the Spirit of counsel and of power, the Spirit of knowledge and of the fear of the LORD ... He will not judge by what he sees with his eyes, or decide by what he hears with his ears ... (Isaiah 11:23)

In other words, he won't rely on his senses to judge how to work in this world, but by what the Spirit tells him — knowledge from another world than this one.

Jesus said that when we face authorities who persecute us for our faith, the Spirit of God will give us the right words to say — words that we wouldn't ordinarily think of on our own. (Mark 13:11) He also promised to send the Spirit to us, who would "guide you into all truth." (John 16:13) The Spirit of God opened Stephen's eyes to see Christ standing at God's right hand when the Jews were stoning him. (Acts 7:55-56) The Spirit tells us what to pray for and how to pray when we don't know. (Romans 8:26) The mystery of Christ "has now been revealed by the Spirit" to the Church." (Ephesians 3:5) Paul said that whoever rejects the teaching of Scripture isn't rejecting man but the Spirit, who is actually doing the teaching. (1 Thessalonians 4:8) The Spirit gives us a taste of the

Heavenly gift, and enlightens us about the world of God. (Hebrews 6:4) The prophets, Peter tells us, always spoke as they were "carried along by the Holy Spirit" — the Spirit told them what to say. (1 Peter 1:21) The Spirit testifies to the cleansing power of Christ's blood. (1 John 5:6) John the apostle was praying in the Spirit when he had his revelation of Christ. (Revelation 1:10) The Spirit says things to the churches of Christ that they need to hear. (Revelation 2:11)

This is just a sampling from the Bible about the work of the Spirit as he reveals the world of God to our minds and souls.

- ***The Spirit gives power.*** "But you will receive power when the Holy Spirit comes on you; and you will be my witnesses in Jerusalem and in all Judea and Samaria, and to the ends of the earth." (Acts 1:8)

The kind of power that this verse is talking about isn't any power that we are familiar with. Simon made that mistake when he saw the Apostles working miracles and tried to buy the power of the Spirit from them. (Acts 8:9-24) The power that the Spirit gives is a new thing, something that this world doesn't know anything about.

The first time that we find the empowering work of the Spirit in the Bible is in Genesis.

In the beginning God created the heavens and the earth. Now the earth was formless and empty, darkness was over the surface of the deep, and the Spirit of God was hovering over the waters (Genesis 1:1-2)

What exactly was there at the beginning, the building blocks that God used to make the world, we don't know; we do know that it was "without form" and "without substance" (as the Hebrew words mean), which are the two necessary characteristics of matter as we know it. In other words, the Spirit brought non-existence into existence; he gave life and substance to what used to be nothing. The earth and plants and animals and man all exist because the Spirit gave us the ability to exist. Without him we would return to nothingness.

That's what happened to the world when the Spirit moved in the beginning. What happens in men's souls? Here is where we need the Spirit most of all, because we are all dead to the world of God from our birth. (Ephesians 2:1-3) Even if we see God (the first job of the Spirit), and even if we know the truth about God and his world, we still can't do anything about it. God requires obedience from us — but we can't obey him because we are so bound up in our sin. He requires faith from us — but we can't believe in him because we are so confused, wandering in this dark world. He calls us to live in his world, but we can't get out of our world. At the very least we are to "love the Lord your God with all our heart and with all your soul and with all your mind," (Matthew 22:37) but unfortunately we aren't interested — there are other things that we love more.

When the Spirit works on the heart, however, that person wakes up to God's world, like opening one's eyes on a bright morning. "Wake up, O sleeper, rise from the dead, and Christ will shine on you." (Ephesians 5:14) He can see things now that he hasn't seen before. Even this dark world that we live in gets a new light: the Spirit shines on our lives, on circumstances, on other people, like a spotlight and shows us things that we couldn't see before.

The Spirit not only wakes us up to the world of God, he makes us *able* to live in God's world. "Flesh and blood cannot inherit the kingdom of God" (1

Corinthians 15:50), simply because the conditions there would kill us. The air is different, the food is different, the light is different (I'm using symbols of the realities, you understand; "air" and "food" and "light" in Heaven are spiritual things, whereas we think of our physical world when we hear those words.) Paul said that before we can hope to rise into Heaven, some things about us have to change:

> So it will be with the resurrection of the dead. The body that is sown is perishable, it is raised imperishable; it is sown in dishonor, it is raised in glory; it is sown in weakness, it is raised in power; it is sown a natural body, it is raised a spiritual body. (1 Corinthians 15:42-44)

In order to live before God and not die, we have to change completely. Our natures as they are now can neither survive before God's glory, nor can we understand or appreciate what we would see there. Our physical senses weren't made to be aware of the things of God. Unless, of course, the Spirit gives life to our souls — our souls *were* made to be aware of God. That's why the Bible talks about having "eyes to see" and "ears to hear." The Spirit makes us alive spiritually (which Jesus called, appropriately, being "born again" — John 3:3) so that our spiritual senses can start picking up on the things of God. In order to pick up the signals from a radio station, you have to first turn the radio on. Before anybody can hope to know God, their souls must be made alive first.

The Spirit makes it possible for us to obey God's commands; without him we could never do it. (Ezekiel 36:26-27) The Law is spiritual, Paul says (Romans 7:14), and the Spirit shows us what God means by his Law and how we are expected to obey it. The Spirit of God blew over the bones in Israel and made them alive again. (Ezekiel 37:1-14) The Lord will build his kingdom "not by might nor by power, but by my Spirit" (Zechariah 4:6); because of this, his kingdom will be eternal and it will consist of things that will satisfy both him and us. Jesus drove out demons by the Spirit of God. (Matthew 12:28) Jesus said that, when someone has the Spirit in him, it will be a spring of water welling up inside to eternal life. (John 4:14) "The Spirit gives life, the flesh counts for nothing" (John 6:63) — and Jesus' words were Spirit because they give us spiritual life, the awareness of God and ability to live for God. Peter, the disciple whom the Jews had last seen denying the Lord, stood up at Pentecost full of the Spirit and preached the eternal Gospel to the Jews — with thousands of conversions as a result. (Acts 2) The Holy Spirit gives joy to God's people. (Romans 14:17) It's because of the Spirit's work that we have faith in Christ — a faith that comprehends the breadth and depth of Christ's person and work. (Ephesians 2:8; 3:16) The Spirit washes and renews us so that we become heirs of God's promises. (Titus 3:5)

A DEPOSIT . . .

This is the work of the Spirit. But now comes the clincher: this same Spirit comes to live in the heart of every believer. This is the way Paul puts it:

> Having believed, you were marked in him with a seal, the promised Holy Spirit, who is a deposit guaranteeing our inheritance until the redemption of those who are God's possession — to the praise of his glory. (Ephesians 1:13)

Instead of having to be content to just read in the Bible *about* the work of the Spirit, each believer can experience the reality of the spiritual power that comes with the Holy Spirit's presence. In fact, if someone doesn't know what it's like — all this business of revelation, knowing when God is near, knowing God's mind on things, being able to please God, and so on — then you can be sure that he doesn't have the Spirit in his heart. The sure sign of the Spirit's presence is his characteristic work in a believer's life.

• *The Spirit makes us spiritually alive.* We can't say that we are spiritually alive unless there really is spiritual life in us. Spiritual life is the same life that Christ has; he *promised* that he would send his Spirit so that we would have the same kind of life that he has. The branches of the vine share the same life as the vine itself. (John 15:1-8) If we have Christ's Spirit, then we will do the same works that Christ did.

Christ is living an *indestructible* life now. The Father raised him from the dead never to die again. There is no power on earth that can touch him anymore; he is no longer subject to the whims and persecuting spirit of the Romans or the Jews or anybody else. Nothing can set him back, nothing can make him fail, nothing can make his joy and peace waver. This is the same life that is in you, through the Spirit of Christ.

Christ is living a *righteous* life now. He never did sin, not even when faced with the temptations of the world and the devil. But he went even further and perfectly fulfilled the righteous requirements of the Law — therefore buying the redemption of his people. He has in his hands a righteousness that will cover any and all sinners, no matter who they are or what they have done. That blazingly righteous life that is in Christ is available to us too, through the Spirit of Christ.

Christ is living *in the presence of God* now. He ascended to the right hand of the throne of God where he lives "to judge the wicked and the dead." He always stands before God to intercede for his people. He is preparing a place for us there, in God's house, where we can live too. He is always with God, never to leave him again, enjoying the treasures of God, loving and being loved.   We also live before God in Christ, through the Spirit of Christ working in us.

What are you capable of now, since the Spirit enables you to be aware of God and his world?   The Spirit helps you understand what it is that God expects from you.   The Spirit changes your heart so that you want to know God; otherwise you would be just like everyone else, more interested in the things in this world.   The Spirit blesses you with the treasures of God's world — not the whole thing, but "tastes" that whet your appetite for more.   Those are the high times, the "mountain top" experiences.   Because of the work of the Spirit in your heart, there are two realities for you now: the world that you were first born into, and God's world.   Now that you know that there *is* another world, and that it's far better than this one, you are willing to leave everything in this one behind you as you look to the city "whose architect and builder is God" (Hebrews 11:10) — that is, if you are living by the Spirit.

• *The Spirit takes us to Heaven.*   This is the part that makes a spiritual life possible.   If we were filled with the Spirit and had no more than that, then the world that we will one day inherit would remain news from a far distant land; interesting, perhaps tantalizing, but not very real yet.   But the Lord pushes one step further and actually brings us to that other world now — through a special miracle of the Holy Spirit.   We can know that God lives and reigns on his throne because we have *seen* him there. (Isaiah 6:7)   We can know that Christ's blood is sufficient for any sin because we have *seen* that blood on the eternal altar, satisfying the requirements of the Law. (Hebrews 12:24)   In fact, that passage from Hebrews is worth quoting here:

> But you have come to Mount Zion, to the Heavenly Jerusalem, the city of the living God. You have come to thousands upon thousands of angels in joyful assembly, to the church of the

firstborn, whose names are written in Heaven.
You have come to God, the judge of all men, to
the spirits of righteous men made perfect, to
Jesus the mediator of a new covenant, and to the
sprinkled blood that speaks a better word than
the blood of Abel. (Hebrews 12:22-24)

This is what the Spirit of God does for you.
You don't have to wait until you die before you see
God and his kingdom; you have a chance to see it *now*,
while you are still in this world, through the special
work of the Spirit of God. Of course you are still
rooted firmly in this world until you die, and those
spiritual treasures are things that you have to be content
to simply look at and taste; you will have to wait for
the full reality of them until you leave this world
behind. But by the grace of God you can *look* into his
kingdom now, to give you hope and encouragement, by
praying in the Spirit.

• *The Spirit helps us pray.* This is a strange new
world that we are getting into, and it's no surprise when
we feel overwhelmed by its reality — we don't exactly
know what to say or do. It's like suddenly finding
yourself playing in the major leagues when you've
always played with children before. What does one say
to the Almighty? How is one supposed to act in the
presence of such an awesome company as is in
Heaven? If you feel like this, then you are starting to
get a correct impression of what you are involved in.

But here is where the empowering Spirit comes
to our rescue. If he would leave us on our own, we
would stammer out something foolish in front of God
and the angels, and turn away embarrassed, and
probably get no answer from God. But he helps us pray
in a way that will be pleasing to the Lord:

In the same way, the Spirit helps us in our
weakness. We do not know what we ought to

pray, but the Spirit himself intercedes for us with groans that words cannot express. And he who searches our hearts knows the mind of the Spirit, because the Spirit intercedes for the saints in accordance with God's will. (Romans 8:26-27)

The Spirit first of all shows us what to say; that is where he reveals the things of God to us so that they become real to us, and they become something that we want to pray about. Second, he gives us the words to say and the strength to say it in the right way. After all, we want God to hear us and answer us, don't we? Then we have to follow his ceremony, his requirements on how to present our requests. Our voices have to take on a spiritual quality so that they will be heard — they have to have power, persuasiveness, genuineness, sinlessness. The Spirit shows us how to do it and he holds our hands, so to speak, as we do it and gives us the strength and wisdom to go through with it. In other words, we get proficient with dealing in the currency of Heaven.

PRAYING IN THE SPIRIT

If this is what the Spirit of God does for us, how then do we pray in the Spirit? What does it look like? What are the steps? The answer lies in how the Spirit works with us, and how he expects us to respond to him. And the key is in Romans 8.

The point of that passage is this: whoever has the Spirit of God in them will demonstrate that they are heirs of God — especially in how they pray. They will ask for, and live for, what God has prepared for his children. The children of a king prepare for their royal futures! Children of criminals often have a life of crime or at least misery waiting for them. Parents pass on what they have to their children, either in inheritance or lifestyle or values, and God is no different with his children. We show that we are God's children when our lives reflect the fact that we are in touch with our Heavenly Father who constantly cares for us. And that happens by means of the Spirit.

• *The Spirit leads us and controls us.* "You, however, are not controlled by the sinful nature but by the Spirit, if the Spirit of God lives in you." (Romans 8:9) This means that you have different priorities in life now. The Spirit is going to make you consider your ways now, whether or not they are pleasing to God; and he is going to bring the Word of God to your attention so that you can think about it and get your life more in line with it. You won't be able to escape God anymore: "Where can I go from your Spirit? Where can I flee from your presence?" (Psalm 139:7)

That inner voice will be with us all our lives. His job is to remind us about God in all circumstances, to open our eyes to the things of God that we need, to teach us the correct meaning of what we read in the Bible, to give us the faith that we need to please God in everything that we do, to crucify the sin in our hearts. He will be our constant companion till the day we die, and even then he will lead us across that last river into God's eternal presence.

Therefore, he intends to help us pray about all these things. He is always there when we pray, controlling our thoughts and desires, turning our hearts and minds to the things of God. If we resist him, and put our eyes on things of this world, then we "grieve" him – that isn't the way he is leading us! If we aren't aware of God's presence when we pray, it isn't the Spirit's fault; our sin clouds our minds so that we can't see him, just as Balaam in his sin couldn't see God as well as his donkey could see him! God's Spirit is always working on us to lead us to God in faith and hope; if we can't see him then we are fighting the leading of the Spirit. But if you pray about what the Spirit has been sent to guide you into, you prove that you have God's Spirit in you.

• *The Spirit gives us spiritual life.* "But if Christ is in you, your body is dead because of sin, yet your spirit is alive because of righteousness." (Romans 8:10) Our physical senses can't deal with the spiritual world; we are creatures of this world and we are doomed to die here. But someone who has the Spirit of God in him is open to God's world: his spiritual senses, the senses of his soul, are fully aware of the sights and sounds of God's spiritual kingdom. He isn't afraid to leave this world because he is familiar with the next one — he has seen it already in a small way, through the Spirit.

Now when someone has seen the world of God, he isn't satisfied with anything in *this* world anymore. He "sets his mind on things above, not on things below." (Colossians 3:2) He doesn't pray about meat and drink, or how he shall be clothed; "the pagans run after all these things" (Matthew 6:32), and our Father in Heaven knows what we need during our stay in this world. But his Spirit guides us into praying for things that are far more important than keeping our bodies fed and clothed: there are critical spiritual matters to pray for, matters in God's kingdom that desperately need answers. These are matters of state — God's glory, the salvation of God's people from their sins, the defeat of all our enemies, the knowledge of God spread through all the earth, the resurrection, faith in Christ for everything we do. These are what we want to pray for when the Spirit is guiding us. These distinguish the prayers of a child of God.

And when we pray like this, the fruit of the Spirit start showing up in what we do and say. Because it is through us, through our lives of obedience and living "by the Spirit", that God will answer these burning issues in our prayers. He will put love in us, and peace, and patience, and joy, and gentleness and the rest of the Spirit's fruit; and that will cause us to cry out to God even more in prayer, and it will make us clean and sanctified vessels that he will feel comfortable about using. He hears the prayers of his righteous ones because they have work to do.

• *The Spirit puts our misdeeds to death.* "If by the Spirit you put to death the misdeeds of the body, you will live." (Romans 8:13) There is much to do here. If you think that you don't have plenty to pray about concerning your own heart of sin, then you under-estimate your capacity to sin. Even the best of us has the ability to sin mightily. The great sinners that we read about in the newspapers are the weak ones; the rest of us have been able to contain those same sins in our hearts and minds and not let them out into the open where they would reveal what we are inside.

But the Spirit intends to kill those sins. The way he is going to do it is the only way that God has provided for getting rid of our sins: to make us come to the altar "sprinkled with blood" and get forgiveness for our sins. The blood of Christ is the only medicine for a sick soul; the power in that blood can "condemn sin" and free us from its bondage.

So someone who prays in the Spirit will be praying about his sins. There is no other way to take care of them but to come to Christ to be saved, and the Spirit isn't going to let us alone until we have taken care of them. The Spirit will show us just how bad our sin really is, how offended God is with it, how powerful the blood of Christ is to forgive us, how willing the Savior is to receive us and help us, and how welcoming the Father is when we confess it. And after showing us all these spiritual realities, he will empower us to come to God and confess our sin and trust in Christ for salvation, things that we couldn't hope to do on our own strength and will. This is all proof that we are praying in the Spirit, and that we are heirs of God's salvation in Christ coming to get what he has freely given us.

- *The Spirit makes us cry to God.* "And by him we cry, Abba, Father." (Romans 8:15)   This is the crowning proof that we have God's Spirit, when we are led by him to come to God for all these things that we need. If God were our enemy, would we ask him for help? If God were just a friend, could we ask him for such total devotion? But if God were really our Father, and we know that he is — we can see that he is through the Spirit — then doesn't it seem reasonable that we would ask him for such personal and powerful answers? If the God to whom "nothing is impossible" were really our Father, isn't that reason to cry to him for everything?

Therefore we pray.   Because the Spirit has shown us that God really is our Father, we pray with all hope and faith. We pray with confidence and boldness. We pray knowing that our Father will hear us and answer us.   We pray humbly because this is God Almighty, and we are encouraged as we pray because he loves us. When we pray like this, with this kind of confidence and insight, then we are praying in the Spirit — we show that we are truly God's children;   we demonstrate our special relationship to him.

THE COROLLARY:

So far we have seen that the Spirit does two things for us in prayer: first, he shows us the spiritual world that God lives in, and makes these things real to us; because of this we will pray with all the more interest for what we see there. Second, he gives us the ability and the power to come to the spiritual God and ask for the things of Heaven. Without him we wouldn't get higher than this world, and we certainly wouldn't be able to receive and use the things of God — not in our ignorance and sinfulness and weakness.

But you may have already realized an important "therefore" to all this. If this is true, if the Spirit transfers us to Heaven during prayer and helps us live in the spiritual atmosphere of God's Heaven for a short time, then something else has to be true. When someone prays "in the Spirit" then he is doing something that no ordinary mortal can ever hope to do on his own, nor would he want to. We can sum it up like this:

If what you say in prayer is something that an unbeliever can understand and want for himself, you are *not* praying in the Spirit of God.

There is a Scripture that states this principle point blank:

We have not received the spirit of the world but the Spirit who is from God, that we may understand what God has freely given us. This is what we speak, not in words taught us by human wisdom but in words taught by the Spirit, expressing spiritual truths in spiritual words. The man without the Spirit does not accept the things that come from the Spirit of God, for they are foolishness to him, and he cannot understand them, because they are spiritually discerned. (1 Corinthians 2:12-14)

This simple test would effectively knock out a lot of what we pray for. At first it may seem too severe to limit what we pray about to only those things that an unbeliever won't accept or understand; what else is left to pray about? We ask for food and shelter, for jobs to support our families, for financial security, for national peace, for health (as we get older, most of our prayers for others are requests for their healing), and a host of other things that we are all very much interested in. But that's precisely the problem: *everyone* is interested in these things. Even unbelievers want these things. And my point isn't that we shouldn't want them too; we live in this world just like anybody else, and when we have the good things of this world we call them "blessings" from God and rightly so.

The problem is that physical "blessings" won't help our souls in the least, and the soul is where we need help. The rich man had every material blessing he wanted in life, and yet he ended up in Hell; poor Lazarus, who had to beg scraps of bread to eat at the rich man's gate, ended up in Heaven. (Luke 16:19-31) Who was "blessed" in the end? The ten lepers came to Jesus for healing, and all ten walked away completely healed. Only one came back for spiritual healing, however. (Luke 17:19) Which of them was really "blessed"? James says that it's the poor among you that God holds in high esteem; the rich among you have spiritual troubles on their hands. (James 1:9-11; 2:5-7) Who is really "blessed" in our churches, then – the rich or the poor?

Even such a simple thing as thanking God for the bread that we eat is loaded with spiritual implications. Do we eat to satisfy our lusts? Did we expect this food from God as our rightful due? Will we use the strength we get from it to sin against him? If so, it would be far better to choke on it! "Man does not live on bread alone, but on every word that comes from the mouth of God." (Matthew 4:4) The kingdom of God doesn't consist of meat and drink, but righteousness, peace, and joy in the Holy Spirit. (Romans 14:17) Our prayer at mealtime shouldn't be just a thanks for food, but for the food that keeps us alive *to live for his glory alone.*

Praying in the Spirit means that you are living in another world than this one, that you hold certain things precious that an unbeliever despises. Your prayers should sound like nonsense to him if you are really praying as you should be. You see things that he doesn't see. You have different opinions on things in this world than he has. He doesn't mind sin; you hate sin. He knows nothing about the true God; you know enough about God to guide you in what to say to God and how to say it. The unbeliever laughs at Heaven; you look forward to it and despise this world's hollow promises. You see? The two of you are on completely different planes of existence when you are at prayer. It's no wonder that he doesn't understand you! Your prayers will be as much different as those of the tax collector and the Pharisee. (Luke 18:14)

AN EXAMPLE PRAYER

The prophet Elijah was a man full of the Holy Spirit. Perhaps his greatest triumph was when he stood against the prophets of Baal, on Mt. Carmel, and challenged them to a duel of the gods. The Baal prophets built an altar and prayed that their god would send fire down from Heaven to burn it up, and Elijah was to do the same. The god who answered, Elijah said, was the real God.

Elijah put his finger on the whole issue of prayer in that challenge. The God who *answers* — he is the real God. False gods don't answer prayers like Elijah's; only the God who lives in Heaven, the God of the Bible, answers prayer like that. Here is Elijah's prayer:

> LORD, God of Abraham, Isaac and Israel, let it be known today that you are God in Israel and that I am your servant and have done all these things at your command. Answer me, O LORD, answer me, so these people will know that you, O LORD, are God, and that you are turning their hearts back again. (1 Kings 18:36-37)

There are several clues about this prayer that show that Elijah was praying in the Spirit of God:

He could see who the real God was. This was the point of the whole exercise: who is the real God? The Israelites were confused; they had been listening to the prophets of Baal and they thought that Baal just may be as real, if not more so, as the Lord. But Elijah knew exactly who the real God was. He could *see* that there was no God but Yahweh. His prayer shows his confidence as he steps up to God's throne and asks for a miracle — something that only the God of Israel can do. There's no doubt in his mind that he is coming to someone who can not only set the sacrifice on fire, but all the water that was poured on it as well! He obviously gloried in the presence of God.

He knew what God wanted him to do. "I am your servant and have done all these things at your command." We can probably assume something here: that Elijah had prayed before this particular moment and had already received God's instructions on exactly what to do with the prophets of Baal. Here we see him reporting back to God, telling him that he carried out his instructions. The point is that Elijah *knew* God's will – his very specific will for this circumstance. Can we claim to know God's will so clearly when we pray? Unless the Spirit enables us to see into God's Temple in Heaven, we grope around during prayer and ask to know God's will without much hope of seeing it in the near future. Elijah, however, had keen spiritual vision: he saw God on the throne. He heard God's voice, he understood his orders, and now he was reporting back to the King with his orders carried out. Such clear, spiritual vision is rare!

He was face to face with God. "Answer me, O LORD, answer me! " We are able to see only Elijah in this story, standing on Mt. Carmel, surrounded by hundreds of false prophets and thousands of Israelites. The scene is striking, even dramatic; but still it's a pretty one-sided conversation that we are listening to. We don't have any visual hint that God is around any more than the doubting Israelites had. But Elijah stands before the God of Heaven. He could see the whole spiritual reality of the thing stretching out to eternity; he could see the throne of God, and *there* is where he took up his position. He was in front of God, and God was in front of him. Like a servant of a king, he came to beg God's answer to his prayer. Isn't it impressive how personal, direct, and familiar he is with God? He fully expects God to hear him and answer him. Such confidence, such boldness, only comes when we clearly see that we are standing before God.

He had boldness to declare his faith in God before the false prophets. Most of us would have cringed at the challenge that Elijah took up. Imagine the scene: if he would have been wrong about God's answer, the prophets of Baal would have surely killed him! And the Israelites would have went home convinced that Yahweh didn't exist, or at least he wasn't as powerful as Baal. Elijah, however, filled with the Spirit, found boldness and confidence to testify to the reality of God – and his miracle-working power – to his enemies and doubters.

He knew what God was doing with the Israelites. Elijah didn't make up any of this stuff himself; he was only obeying God's orders. He could see what God was up to, and why the Lord had put together this whole affair. He could see that God was about to deal a mortal blow to Baal worship, and that he was stretching out his hand to reclaim some of his people to himself. Elijah knew what was going on spiritually between God and his people. We very rarely pray with such spiritual insight. Often we only know long after the fact what God was doing; but while we are in the fire of affliction we are usually just as confused as everyone else as to what to pray for. But Elijah could see it all before it happened! The only possible way that you can know ahead of time what God will do is if you see it done in Heaven, before God does it on earth. That only comes from praying in the Spirit.

SUGGESTED PRACTICE

Unfortunately we can't turn the Spirit on and off at our pleasure. The Spirit "blows where it wills," and we can't any more dictate the moving of the Spirit than what Simon the magician hoped to do with his money. Therefore it would seem pretty hopeless that we could pray in the Spirit on all occasions and in all kinds of prayers and requests, whenever we want to. How in the world can we *make sure* that our prayers are in the Spirit when the Spirit only does what he wills?

The will of the Lord, however, isn't so mysterious and elusive. His will is that you be saved; that you come into his presence and worship him; that you prepare yourself for adoption into his family; that you take on the image of Jesus Christ; that you know God better. His will concerning you is very pointed and direct. And the way he intends to do all this to you is through his Spirit.

Therefore listen to the Spirit when you pray. There is a lot he wants to do with you, and if you are open to his leading then you will find yourself praying "in the Spirit" more often.

• *Listen to the Spirit as he convicts you of sin.* When you read the Word (as you *should* be doing when you pray!) the Spirit is going to stab your heart with it. The Word of God is the truth, and you need to hear it. There is much in your life that isn't right, and God wants to deal with you about it. As you read, don't avoid the painful parts; don't skip the parts that describe the life of a righteous man. Don't assume, when the Bible talks about sin and sinners, that it's not referring to you! Let the Spirit search your soul and expose you to the eyes of God who sees and knows all. When the Word opens you up like this for God's inspection, you are in the best possible position for prayer: the Spirit is holding you up before God, and it's then that you need to present your requests to the Father who can forgive you and cleanse you. Don't avoid times like that; long for them.

• *Listen to the Spirit as he points you to Christ.* God made Christ to be our spiritual medicine, our inexhaustible supply for all our needs. But it isn't apparent to the eyes of flesh that he is: the Jews despised him, the Romans scoffed at him, kings of the earth laugh at his crown of thorns, and even today's Christians seem to have better things to do than to sit at his feet and learn from him. But when you see something in Christ that feeds your soul, that's a sure sign that the Spirit of Christ is opening your eyes to his glory. Go for it. Reach out and take what the Spirit is helping you to see. Accept the leading of the Spirit as he takes you by the hand and leads to the only one who can help you, no matter what your problem or need. The more that you see that Christ is your "all in all", your spiritual storehouse where you should be spending more of your waking hours, then the more you will be praying in the Spirit.

• *Listen to the Spirit as he makes God's world real.* Prayer, after all, shouldn't be an empty ceremony. If it really is coming into God's presence in Heaven, then shouldn't something seem real about the whole thing? At the very least we should know that we are in God's presence, even if we aren't aware of anything else that surrounds him there. But the Spirit will make these things real as we read about them and meditate on them: the "city of the living God", where there are thousands of angels worshipping him, and the spirits of righteous men bowing down to him. You will sometimes see the sprinkled blood of Christ glistening on the altar in front of God. You will know that you are one of an uncounted multitude who stand before God in prayer. This isn't your imagination, not if you come to the Lord in Truth (his Word) and follow the Spirit as he leads you unerringly to God in the right way. The Spirit will show us what we need at the time of prayer. The promise is that "they will all know God, from the least to the greatest." It is your privilege — and it is both possible and necessary — to come before God in the Spirit.

PRAY WITH FAITH

But when he asks, he must believe and not doubt.
(James 1:6)

Christians are probably best characterized by their faith. We are called the "believers" — "All the believers were together ..." "As for the Gentile believers, we have written to them ..." "Set an example for the believers ..." "Love the brotherhood of believers ..."

The point of these and many more Scriptures isn't that Christians are the only people who believe anything. Everyone believes *something* — unfortunately not everyone believes the right thing, though. Christians believe the Truth, recorded in the Bible and made flesh in the person and work of Christ. Their beliefs set them apart from all other systems of doctrine in the history of man. When the Bible calls them "believers," then, it means that they believe what God wants them to believe – they believe the only truth. Everyone else is mistaken.

But is this all there is to faith? Is it enough that you believe the right doctrines about God and man and salvation? Obviously not, because there are many people who have all this truth down pat and yet their souls are still dead to God. They can't sense the reality of Heaven. Though they can quote chapter and verse from the Bible, they don't have any personal experience of the spiritual life that are in the words they know mentally. *What* you believe is only half the story of true faith.

Even born-again Christians, however, fall short of "living by faith," as Paul puts it. We love our Bibles, but we aren't necessarily men and women of faith just because we know the truth. More often than not we struggle with unbelief, with discouragement and depression, with sins that we should have overcome long ago, with this world's lies and deceits, with fear of all the powers that surround us. For instance, we think it's perfectly natural to be terrified of a raging storm — Jesus, however, marveled at the disciples' unbelief. (Matthew 8:26)

Prayer is like a weather vane in this respect. A vane will point in the direction that the wind is blowing, and we put it on the roof so that we can best tell the wind's direction — the air blows freely up there and not so freely along the ground. If a person is living by faith, as the Scriptures tell us how, then it will show up best during a prayer. Prayer is when we climb above the clutter of this world and get into the spiritual atmosphere of Heaven; when we pray, we are dealing with spiritual matters and (as we saw in the previous chapter) we actually come into God's presence. If we have any faith at all, it will show up clearly in our prayers. Faith will inevitably point our souls to God; unbelief will steer us away from him.

This means that we will live as we pray. If we pray in faith, we can't help but live by faith. If we don't have faith when we pray, then we won't have the faith to live for God.

We want to look now at the kind of faith that the Bible talks about. What people often take for faith is a weak substitute of the powerful reality that God has given his people. True spiritual faith that God gives will transform your way of living and praying. It will put new words in your mouth and move you to ask for things that men haven't dared to imagine taking. It will widen the scope of your prayers so that all of Heaven will lie before you, and all the promises of God, and you will find the courage and strength to pick up what you want and use it in your life. A little bit of true faith is enough to move the heart of God in your favor.

Jesus taught us that faith has this characteristic of massive power; even a little bit, he assured us, is enough to move mountains of problems with absolutely no effort at all.

I tell you the truth, if you have faith as small as a mustard seed, you can say to this mountain, "Move from here to there" and it will move. Nothing will be impossible for you. (Matthew 17:20)

Faith has an inner spring of power that shatters all the barriers that this world tries to throw in its way. Tap this power of faith, Jesus told us, and nothing you ask will be denied you.

WHAT IS FAITH?

There has been some confusion about the words "faith" and "believe." Some think that they are two different concepts; but that's not true. Both words come from the same Greek root "πιστ-" — "pisteuo," meaning "to believe" or "have faith," and "pistis," meaning "faith" or "belief." The two English words come from the same Greek word.

And there has been a lot of confusion about what the word "faith" means. Perhaps we need to look now at the Bible's definition for it:

Now faith is being sure of what we hope for and certain of what we do not see. (Hebrews 11:1)

Everyone knows this verse by heart; but maybe we don't understand it as well as we are able to quote it. There is a lot between the lines here! We have to pull together many other teachings from Scripture in order to grasp what the writer is actually saying about the nature of faith. In light of some other truths that we can find in the Bible, let's put it another way:

Faith is living in the light of God's world.

Let's unpack this into a few principles that will help us see the startling nature of true faith.

- *We need the impossible.* If man were content with this world then there wouldn't be any need for Heaven; but when a person becomes a Christian, he suddenly finds a distaste for this world and a longing for God's world.   The old works, the old friends, the old pleasures, the old moral systems just don't satisfy the inner longing for something solid that is worth living for. What we need now are eternal treasures.

Suddenly we find that our old way of living leaves a lot of problems unsolved. Why is man always at war? Why is there such widespread greed and selfishness? Why do societies struggle unsuccessfully to keep the peace? Why is there so much suffering and death? You would think that the more sophisticated and technologically advanced our civilization gets, the better our world would become. You would think that people are happier now that their riches are increased. But the ideals are always beyond our reach no matter how hard we try; this world just wasn't made to satisfy us.

Add to those problems the ones that God creates for us — all the demands of the Law, the perfect example of manhood in Christ that we have to be like, the expectations that he has for the perfect Church, the balance between good deeds and faith, the necessity of the fruit of the Spirit being seen in everything we do and say, the requirement that we glorify God in everything — and now it all seems out of our reach; even being a Christian looks impossible. How can we possibly do anything to help the world with its problems? Is it possible to be everything that God expects us to be?

Most people simply bow out at this stage. They feel like they weren't called to solve the world's problems, and God doesn't expect perfection from them; so they don't worry about it anymore. But the problem with that "solution" is that the world continues in its sin and suffering and dying while Christians look on apathetically (or helplessly).   And Christians themselves often live in a way that God is not at all pleased with.

The situation in the world and the Church is desperate. We need answers – good answers, not the old ones that men have been trying for thousands of years and failing with. If we don't get some help soon then more people are going to die in their misery and sin, and we will end up being one of the most unprofitable generations in the history of the Church. The enemies of God have rarely been stronger than they are now; even if we mount up an attack against the powers that keep men in darkness and sin, we can't hope to win against them. They have hold of the political, economic, educational, and even religious systems with a grip that we don't know how to deal with. We need something from God — in other words, a miracle.

• *To God, nothing is impossible.* "Dealing With Impossibilities" is the name of God's business. The things that defeat us are no problem to him. "With man this is impossible, but not with God; all things are possible with God." (Mark 10:27) "For nothing is impossible with God." (Luke 1:37)

We are so used to living in defeat that we think that defeat is normal. We pray not for miracles but simply to maintain the status quo, that things don't get any worse than they are already. Miracles sound nice, but they only happened to people a long time ago. God must work differently now in our own time.

But that's not true at all. We have the same God that Abraham had, and Moses and Samuel and David and Elijah and Hezekiah and all the other people who saw the Lord move in amazing ways. The problem with us is that we haven't gotten a good view of God yet and therefore we have such little faith.

Here is what you would see if you could see God:

The LORD is a warrior;   the LORD is his Name.
Pharaoh's chariots and his army he has hurled
into the sea . . . Your right hand, O LORD, was
majestic in power. Your right hand, O LORD,
shattered the enemy. (Exodus 15:3-4,6)

The LORD is my Shepherd, I shall lack nothing.
He makes me in down in green pastures, he
leads me beside quiet waters, he restores my
soul. He guides me in paths of righteousness
for his Name's sake. (Psalm 23:1-3)

Meditate on these two passages for a few
minutes. What would you say if the Lord suddenly
came into your life and threw your enemies around like
that? What if he lifted you out of your troubles, to a
safe place, and fought your battles for you — and won
them all? What if the Lord gently took you in his arms,
like a tender shepherd with a lamb, and carried you for
a while? What if he fed you and watered you with the
bliss of Heaven, with peaceful and loving words, and
gave your heart rest from your daily trials?

You would probably be stunned. You probably
haven't had things like that happen to you for quite a
long while, if ever. You've probably gotten so used to
living without God that you think it couldn't possibly
come true; all these promises in the Scripture couldn't
be for you.

And yet this is exactly what God does for
people. He does the impossible; he does miracles that
upset this world's powers. He flicks his enemies away
like they were so much dust in the wind; he pours out
blessed peace and happiness from Heaven like
floodwaters. There is no end to the joy that he can
give. He is full of forgiveness and compassion, enough
for the greatest sinner. He can bring the dead back to
life with just a command. He can make a few loaves of
bread feed thousands of people. With a rebuke he

brings a raging storm to a dead halt. He restores the mind of the insane and delivers them from demons. We just can't list all the kinds of miraculous works that God is capable of doing, all the way from his terrifying wrath to the tender compassion of a Father; he is able to do anything we need.

The problem isn't that he *can't* do the miraculous — the problem is that we don't believe that he *will*. Once you see the Lord for yourself you won't doubt his ability again. The purpose of the miracles of Jesus was to convince people that he was God's Son. This brought them out by the thousands; they wouldn't leave him alone until he did a miracle for them too. All the stories in the Bible that tell us the amazing miracles of God, both physical miracles and miracles of the heart and soul, are designed to convince you that he is able to help you with anything. There is nothing he can't do for us, and the proof is there in his written Word.

But you should beware of something when you begin to look at God: this world is going to start throwing smoke screens in front of your eyes, to prevent you from seeing the glory of God. "That's impossible," it will say to you; "no rational, common-sense person would ever believe that stuff." A world in six days? Impossible! Science can tell you why it is clearly not true. Salvation through the blood of Jesus? Impossible! No man can die for another; we all have to make our own way to Heaven. Loving your enemy? Impossible! You have to draw the line somewhere; you can't just be a doormat. On and on the world will argue, showing how the Bible just can't be true.

Faith, however, will tear through these outward appearances of "reasonableness" and "wisdom" and enter into God's Temple where the real truth is. Faith doesn't get fooled by the appearances of this world; it knows that the "impossible" world of God is the only possible way that this world will ever get straightened out. That's why we said that faith is living in the light of God's world. We enter, through the Spirit (remember the last chapter?), into God's presence and see him. We can see who he really is, as we read his Word. That sight makes us confident in his powers, and his good will toward us. And that light from Heaven shines on our lives here on earth, showing up the emptiness of this world and how much more certain God's promises are than any of the lies and hollow promises of this world.

We need the truth of God to defeat the lies of this world; we need the power of God to put down the impotence of this world. We need success for a change, not the failure, that we are so used to, that comes from living the way this world tells us to live. It's about time we closed our ears to the world's arguments and started believing in the God who does the impossible.

• *Consider it done.* God's honor is at stake here. If he said he would do something, then he's going to do it; he never breaks his promises. Faith gets a hold of the utter dependability of God's Word and refuses to let go.

God promised that what he said he would do, he *will* do. We have a lot of problems with his promises mainly because we have seen so few of them come true. We say that he hasn't done what he promised *yet* — so can we really expect miracles from him *now*? Probably there are two reasons why he hasn't given us some of the things we've asked for: *first*, he never promised some of the things that we think he promised us; we got it wrong. He never promised every Christian a free bag of groceries, or success as this world defines success. He did promise us that he will be there to provide for us when we are hungry, and will sustain us when we fail in the world's eyes and suffer humiliation. But he never said he would always keep us out of those troubles. Sometimes troubles make good discipline for our souls.

Second, sometimes he gets offended with our lack of faith and simply moves on somewhere else. We don't get what we want because we don't really think he will fulfill his promise to us. This cuts straight to his heart. His honor is at stake here: he is either a God who keeps his Word or he is not. Which is it? Will you accuse him of lying? Will you accuse him of not being able to do what he promised? Are you ready to stand before Heaven and earth and testify to his inability to keep his Word? It's no wonder, then, that God doesn't do things for people when they slander his name (which is what they are doing when they don't believe in him). "And he did not do many miracles there because of their lack of faith." (Matthew 13:58)

On the other hand, a person who believes in God is like a little child: there simply isn't any doubt in his mind that God will do what he promised. He just waits for it to happen. Abraham knew, even though God told him to sacrifice his son Isaac, that God was going to make a great nation through the descendants of his son. He didn't know how God would do it, but we don't have to know *how* God will work a miracle — just believe that he can and will. A simple, child-like faith can go back to everyday life knowing that the realities that we hope for will eventually come to pass.

Nothing can shake that inner confidence. When God has spoken, the believer can stand against anything in full assurance that God is behind him. David faced Goliath alone with just a sling and a few pebbles because he knew already that Goliath was history. "It is not by sword or spear that the LORD saves; for the battle is the LORD's, and he will give all of you into our hands." (1 Samuel 17:47)

There are many examples of this kind of faith in the Bible. In each case we can see the same unique characteristics that inevitably come with faith: God promises the impossible, because nothing else will do the job; the believer brushes aside the appearances, and the wisdom of the world, that claim such a thing could never happen; he enters into God's world through faith and sees that God can and will do what he promised; and, finally, he goes back to life assured of the fact that he will see those promises fulfilled.

Moses — When Moses met God at the burning bush he was 80 years old, wanted in Egypt for murder, and working as a shepherd in the land of Midian — he was essentially a nobody. He was hardly a promising candidate for leading the Israelites to the Promised Land! But God had his own plans in mind, and he picked Moses to do the job. Never mind that the Israelites were under the thumb of one of the most powerful rulers in the world, never mind that Moses' demand was laughable ("Let my people go!"), never mind that the Israelites had no way to defend themselves from Pharaoh's soldiers and no way across the impenetrable Red Sea, never mind that there was no support system for them out in the desert wilderness, never mind that the inhabitants of Canaan fully intended to defend their homes and pastures from these outsiders — never mind that the whole thing, from first to last, was the most impossible thing that anybody ever dreamed up! This is what God wanted to do, and Moses believed him. Moses knew that God *could* do all this and he knew that God *would* do all this. There was no other workable plan for getting them to the Promised Land. Watch Moses as he faces Pharaoh, as he leads the Israelites to the shores of the Red Sea, as he brings them to Mt. Sinai, as he leads them through the wilderness, as he brings the nation to the borders of Canaan. Here was a man who was convinced of the sureness of God's promises in spite of all the appearances to the contrary; he just kept going the way God told him to go.

David — Samuel anointed David when he was still a shepherd boy working for his father Jesse. Nobody at the time believed that this "runt" of the family would amount to anything; even Samuel was surprised that the Lord picked David from among his older, more impressive brothers. But this was only the beginning of David's struggle to the throne. Saul, the king in power, grew to hate David – he could see that the Lord favored David and he was jealous. So starts a long story of the hunt for the "outlaw." David wandered in the Judean wilderness for years and evaded Saul's army, sometimes even going over to the Philistine camp to escape from his fellow Israelites! Nobody could have predicted that this renegade, this nobody, this man with a price on his head, would one day be the shining star of Israelite history and the very picture of the Messiah. Except David himself, that is. Read some of his psalms as he pours out his heart to God; he *knew* that God was leading him, that one day he would be king, that the impossible would happen. And he knew what God was planning for Israel under David's future reign; he was willing to be an outcast for the time being in order to see those blessings in the future.

Hezekiah — After the Northern tribes were hauled off to Assyria and several kings of the Southern tribes almost prompted the Lord to send them away as well, Hezekiah became king in Jerusalem. He was not of the same stripe as some of his fathers; he was a man of faith. The Lord put that faith to the test once and demonstrated again that he does the impossible for his people. When the people of Jerusalem displeased the power-hungry Assyrians, they sent their best army commander, with a huge army, to either bring Jerusalem to her knees in submission or reduce her to rubble. The city was surrounded, the Assyrian commander stood outside the city walls and mocked Israel's "helpless" God, and the people all looked to Hezekiah for a solution. Now what should they do? He did the only thing he *could* do as a believer — he turned to God for a miracle. The next day there were 185,000 dead men in the Assyrian camp! (2 Kings 18:17 — 19:37)

Paul — Paul was a man of amazing faith, but you have to read his story to appreciate what he was up against. Virtually single-handedly he started churches in several countries, in many cities, against the opposition of angry Jews, in the face of violent persecution from pagans; he was shipwrecked and hungry many times, savagely beaten many times, and opposed, of all things, by his own brother Christians back in Jerusalem. His task was staggering; several times he went to the Lord desperate for a solution to the impossible odds against him. But what carried him through was the vision he had of a great spiritual reality: that God had called him to be the apostle to the Gentiles, that God was going to form his Church out of these "rejected" people. This certainty that the Lord was going to do what he said is what kept Paul going.

THE STEPS OF FAITH

Because faith is such a critical thing to have, the Lord doesn't want us to be in any confusion about what faith actually is and how one goes about exercising faith. He gave us a wonderfully clear example of the process of faith in the story of Abraham. Abraham stepped through, as it were, the separate stages of true faith as God requires it to be.

In fact, the Bible says that Abraham is the model for our faith. His experience wasn't unique to himself or something that only worked in the Old Testament times. Paul calls him "the father of us all" (Romans 4:16) — that is, God did with Abraham exactly what he wants to do with *every believer in the Church*. Abraham's life and faith was a pattern that we must use to judge the genuineness of our own faith. If our faith looks just like Abraham's faith, then God will also "credit it" to us "as righteousness." (Romans 4:3)

"What then shall we say that Abraham, our forefather, discovered in this matter?" (Romans 4:1)

• *Hear the Word of God.* You must start here. Abraham started on his life of faith when he heard God speak to him: "Leave your country, your people and your father's household and go to the land I will show you." (Genesis 12:1) Abraham's faith was based on God's Word.

Abraham's problem was that he had no son. He was an old man when he left his native country, and his wife Sarah was too old to have children anymore. He had pretty much given up on the idea of having any sons of his own, and he was getting ready to leave his entire estate to his chief servant. But God had other plans. He promised Abraham that he would have a son by his wife Sarah — as impossible as this sounded — and his descendants would become a nation, inheriting the land of Canaan.

You can see the process here: Abraham's problem, God's solution. That's the first step of true faith. If we come up with our own solutions to our problems then we cannot expect anything more than what this world promises — its answers don't last, they don't satisfy, and they don't change us for the better. But if we get God's promises, his solutions, then there is no limit to what God will do. He draws from the treasures of Heaven to answer our prayers.

Some people seem to think that they can believe whatever they like and God will honor it. They ask God for things that he never promised to give them; they expect God to do things that he doesn't do. If they would just check the Bible to see what God *did* promise us, and to see the kinds of things that God does, they would quit asking him for foolish things. They would put their hearts on the spiritual realities in God's Temple, things that God specially set up for our salvation. They would look into Christ and see what it is that God has freely given us. These are the only things that are worth asking for; the Lord knows what will help us.

- *Set your heart on it.* Here is the test of true faith: do we really want what God offers us, or are we just playing games — do we pray just to stay on God's good side? You see, the things of God are of such a nature that they alienate unbelievers and charm believers. The enemies of God definitely do not want the treasures of Heaven, and the children of God look forward to it as their inheritance.

Abraham *wanted* what God promised him. He walked away from family, friends, job opportunities, community honors, national benefits, and everything else that filled his world back in Ur. He headed off across the desert to claim God's promise. He considered all the riches of this world, all its honors, and all of its promising future, as of little worth. On the bare Word of God he left it all behind. Obviously he felt that what God was offering him was of infinitely greater worth.

True faith leaves the world behind. There isn't anything here worth dying for. God's promises draw a line between what God wants to give us and what the world tries to give us: unfortunately (or fortunately!) it is always an either/or situation. If you want God's wisdom then you have to turn your back on the world's wisdom and look like a fool. If you want to save your life for eternity then you have to lose it here. If you want riches of Heaven, you have to give away your earthly riches. If you want to be part of the family of God, then you should expect to be alienated from your earthly family — if they won't follow you to Heaven, that is. The reason that the two systems are so opposed to each other is that each claims to answer the special needs of your life — but only one really does. The world ends up to be a cheat in the end.

True faith cherishes the things of God. A person doesn't regret choosing God's ways if he really has faith. He finds that the spiritual treasures that he inherited are worth more than all the world; these are eternal treasures, things that satisfy the soul, things that will last. He can calmly face the loss of everything he has here on earth because he knows what lies in store for him in Heaven. He enjoys the foretaste of the things of God and takes advantages of those seasons of spiritual refreshment, often taking time out from the daily schedule in order to do it. Others wonder why he takes this "religion" business so seriously, but they don't know what he knows: this "religion" is far more real than they realize, and he's enjoying it *now*, like Mary sitting at Jesus' feet. (Luke 10:38-42) They are the ones missing out.

• *Face the impossibility of it.* Here is something that we often fail to do when we try to live by faith. It's no use shutting your eyes to the fact that what God promises is, quite simply, impossible. In fact, in order to appreciate the full value of the promise, you have to fully understand its impossibility!

Abraham, Paul said, "faced the fact that his body was as good as dead — since he was about a hundred years old – and that Sarah's womb was also dead." (Romans 4:19) He knew that there was no earthly way that he could have a son. He couldn't ignore the fact. But instead of depressing him, it was a crucial step in his faith. He saw clearly that God's promise addressed those problems for which there is no human answer.

God isn't interested in doing the possible; he leaves those things for us to do. He goes after the impossible, the unreasonable, the "foolish," the irrational, the undesirable, the unfavorable. He loves waiting until the situation is beyond hope. When we are usually jumping up and down in impatience, wondering how long he could possibly wait until delivering us or helping us, he is just settling down for an even longer wait. Abraham waited 25 years after moving to Canaan until Isaac was finally born. It's as if the Lord wanted the situation to be so impossible that it was laughable to imagine that it could ever happen. In fact, his son's name, Isaac, means "he laughs."

The reason that it's healthy for us to face the impossibility of what God promises is because it takes our hopes completely off ourselves. If we weren't convinced that it was beyond our capacity to do ourselves, we wouldn't need God, would we? If we thought that we were able to live a holy life without God's help, we wouldn't ask him to help. If we thought we could he happy without him, we wouldn't ask him for the treasures of Heaven. But faith gets disgusted with the way the world tries to find happiness apart from God; there is no such thing. And there is no such thing as living a good life apart from God; faith knows that it is impossible and that only God can make us good. In other words, when we are convinced that we can't do this thing, then we will finally turn to the only one who can.

• *Trust in God to do the impossible.* Once you've seen that there's no hope in this world for even the simplest of your needs, the next step is to turn to God and ask him to do the impossible for you. Abraham simply believed that God would give him a son, as wild as that may have sounded to everyone else.

Our faith isn't true faith unless we are trusting God to do what we can't do for ourselves. God is the God of miracles: he makes mountains move, valleys lift up, the dead come to life, the blind to see, the lame to walk, the lost to be saved, the simple to become wise. When John the Baptist wondered if Jesus was the Messiah that was promised, Jesus sent word back as proof of his office:

Go back and report to John what you have seen and heard: The blind receive sight, the lame walk, those who have leprosy are cured, the deaf hear, the dead are raised, and the good news is preached to the poor. Blessed is the man who does not fall away on account of me. (Luke 7:22-23)

This was, in Christ's opinion, proof of his office. God's people ought to realize that their God isn't like the gods of other nations; those gods can't do anything more than send rain during the rainy season and food during harvest – things we would have expected *without* a god's help. Our God, however, sends rain during drought and food during famine! Remember Gideon's fleece that he set before God? He asked for an impossible answer and got it! (Judges 6:36-40) This proved to him that it was the God of Israel who was calling him out to work.

God gets great honor and glory by doing what nobody else can do.

• ***Don't try it yourself.*** Abraham slipped up once. His faith wavered; he began to think that maybe God didn't exactly mean to work such a *miraculous* miracle after all. He took his wife Sarah's advice and had a son by her handmaid Hagar, thinking that this son would qualify as the promise that God originally made to him.

He was wrong. When God promises the impossible, he means the *impossible* — not what we are capable of doing. The Lord alone must do his work, and he doesn't want our solutions. Even if matters get so ridiculously out of hand that we think that something has to give, he wants us to trust him to do it in his own way.

Our answers aren't sufficient to save us. We've already tried for many years living according to our own wisdom and strength, and failed in the attempt. We got no closer to Heaven and real life with all our efforts. The last thing that God wants from us is to go back to that old way of living. He wants us to live a new way from now on: in the power of God, in the wisdom of God, in the kingdom of God, in obedience and faith to him.

Trying to solve your problems by yourself, by your own efforts, according to your own wisdom and ways, is called *salvation by works*. Instead of trusting God to do things for you, you jump the gun (for whatever "good" reasons) and do it on your own. You will find that you aren't going to get anywhere. Real life comes from Christ's hand, not in what you do. Nothing you do will last, nothing you do will help yourself or others in the long run, nothing you do will honor the Lord in the least. The kingdom of God has to be, from first to last, the work of God alone; because only then will it be made out of eternal building materials and built in a way that will please God.

• *Wait on God to do it.* This is perhaps the hardest part of faith: waiting. Abraham waited for 25 years for his son. Others had to wait their entire lifetimes, and even then didn't always get what God promised them. (Hebrews 11:39-42)

Now waiting doesn't mean that you give up asking. If you long for the things of God then you aren't going to quit praying about them. The widow pounded on the judge's door until he got up and gave her what she wanted. (Luke 18:1-8) Jesus counseled us to keep asking and never give up; he wants to see if we really do want these things.

But God will often use time in the process of prayer. He will rarely give us an answer on the spot.

There is much that he is doing in his kingdom, and our request — though extremely important to us and to him — is only one piece in the vast puzzle of the world's affairs. Often it's the case that someone else isn't ready yet, and that's why the Lord is waiting to answer our prayer. Or perhaps the conditions aren't right yet — if he answered right now, it would look too easy and nobody would be impressed with the Lord's power. Or maybe our hearts aren't yet spiritually ready to eat the rich food of Heaven. Whatever the case may be, an answer may be long in coming.

But faith proves itself when it is content to wait. After all, isn't God's promise worth waiting for? Isn't our problem so severe that only God's answer will do — and therefore we *must* wait? Do we have any other hope or help? You can tell whether someone has true faith: they are willing to wait on God to the bitter end — and beyond.

WHY FAITH?

Faith is a particularly appropriate part of prayer for several reasons. **First**, you have no other options. You shouldn't be praying for anything in this world anyway! If you want the things of God, especially while you are still in this world, then you are asking for things that the world will fight against to the death. Everything and everyone of this world are hostile to the things of God; you're going to need a miracle before you start seeing his promises become realities in your life. The Spirit has to clear out some sin and unbelief in your own heart, and push back the enemy from your front door, and arm you for the inevitable conflict. God's promises are free to all who will ask for them, but expect hard labor to get them and keep them. But for those who can push through the hardship and false appearances and humiliation that comes with following Jesus, and reach for the impossible in God's world, there will be peace and victory and joy in the end.

Second, faith pleases God. He loves it when his people trust him so completely to do things for them. That honors him; we say to him, and to whoever might be looking, that *only* God can save, *only* God can bless, *only* God can give strength and wisdom, *only* God can direct our ways, *only* God can protect us. And we throw in our lot with the Lord to the extent that we accept whatever he has for us and wait for him to do it as he wants it done in our lives. A trust like that is rare for us; sometimes we are enabled to trust God completely for a single thing, but we can't seem to get the ball rolling and trust him for everything like that. He wants more faith from us, however. He wants a people of faith who live by faith.

Third, faith shows where our hearts really are. If we don't have any faith then no amount of prayer will move God to answer us. If we aren't convinced that he is faithful to his promises, then evidently we think he is faithless. If our prayers are more ceremony than real, if we don't ask for things that will rock the world back on its heels in the face of God's reality, then evidently we are planning to live life without God. But if our prayers reach out to take hold of the treasures that God has promised to all of his children then it is obvious that we are sick of this world's treasures, that we want a change in our lives, that we want the power of God to push away our enemies and lift us up above the principalities and powers that want to control us. Faith shows the state of our souls.

Fourth, faith makes God's world real in the here and now. Sometimes it's a drab world that we have to live in; it can get pretty discouraging watching unbelievers strut around as if there is no God, and injustice fills the land, and the poor get pushed further down, and the people of God are despised, and Christians live such discouraged lives. Faith brings a breath of fresh air into God's people: with it we know that God is in control, that the wicked may have their day now but their doom is coming. Faith fills our hearts with hope in the inheritance that God has waiting for us. Through faith we hear God speak to us now, in this wilderness, with assurances and guidance. Through faith we can see God's works as he organizes this world according to his preferences, getting everything ready for the final day when all that we have been hoping for will come true.

Last, faith is a wonderful testimony to God. What most impresses unbelievers is when we trust completely in God, in the face of all trials and obstacles and appearances. They are so curious as to what motivates us that they will often ask us, "What makes you so certain of what you are doing?" That's an opportunity to show them that we have a God who is faithful. They can see, by our confidence, that God *does* keep his Word. When God gets glory like that then our faith is doing what the Lord designed it to do: to adorn the Name of God in such a way that it will attract men and women like sweet perfume, to the only one who can save them from sin and death. Nobody else deserves such utter and complete confidence.

PRAYING IN FAITH

We had to look at faith pretty closely because it's such a critical function of a Christian's life. It's not something that we only do in prayer; we have to "live by faith." (Romans 1:17) "Without faith it is impossible to please God." (Hebrews 11:6) We get our very righteousness through the act of faith.

The point is that when we come to pray, we should already be living by faith. Prayer is asking for the miracles of God that we will then get up and wait for in faith. As James says, prayer isn't prayer until you are already believing that God will do his miraculous work in your life.

> But when he asks, he must believe and not doubt, because he who doubts is like a wave of the sea, blown and tossed by the wind. That man should not think that he will receive anything from the Lord; he is a double-minded man, unstable in all he does. (James 1:6-7)

So, everything we've seen about faith can easily be applied to prayer. This is the frame of mind that God wants us in when we pray — believing, confident, expectant, wise to his ways, not satisfied with anything less than his miracles, not put off by the world's counter-arguments. If we are in any other frame of mind, we aren't praying in faith and God won't answer us. What should we keep in mind about faith when we pray? What does faith do for us when we pray?

- *It gives us boldness, confidence.* Without faith, we are afraid to push ourselves into God's presence, not knowing how he will receive us or whether he will answer us. Who knows but what he may send us away without an answer, being too busy to attend to us? But faith changes the picture entirely: it is like coming into a room where everyone is expecting you.

> Therefore, brothers, since we have confidence to enter the Most Holy Place by the blood of Jesus, by a new and living way opened for us through the curtain, that is, his body, and since we have a great high priest over the house of God, let us draw near to God with a sincere heart in full assurance of faith, having our hearts sprinkled to cleanse us from a guilty conscience and having our bodies washed with pure water. Let us hold unswervingly to the hope we profess, for he who promised is faithful. (Hebrews 10:19-23)

A believer can see the road to Heaven. When everyone else is confused, wondering how to find God and how to get him to listen to them, the believer simply goes through the door marked "For Official Use Only" and there he is, in God's presence. He knows that the Lord will immediately put everything down and talk to him. It may seem arrogant to think that God would place such importance on a person's prayers, but we are basing that assumption on the Lord's invitation. He wants us to come to him, he wants to share his riches with us, he wants us to be part of the most important work that he is doing. He calls us "fellow workers" (1 Corinthians 3:9) and calls us in to share his secrets with us. He tells us things that he wouldn't tell anybody else. A man of faith has the right of entry into God's war room as one of God's lieutenants, privy to

God's plans and strategies, called to carry out God's orders. He not only has the *right* of entry to God's presence, he is *expected.*

● *Pray for big things.* Little people have their minds on little, unimportant things; important people concern themselves, however, with great matters. People who don't know God concern themselves with things of this world; God's people, however, are busy with matters of Heaven.

> So do not worry, saying, "What shall we eat?" or "What shall we drink?" or "What shall we wear?" For the pagans run after all these things, and your Heavenly Father knows that you need them. But seek first his kingdom and his righteousness, and all these things will be given to you as well. (Matthew 6:31-33)

In most businesses there are those employees who sweep the floors and answer the telephone, and then there are those who make the policy decisions that guide the entire company. Now some people are perfectly content to sweep floors and answer telephones; they don't want an administrative job — which is fine in matters of everyday life. A lot of people aren't cut out to do more complex jobs! But when we get into the world of the Spirit the lines of division change completely — the floor sweeper is now the administrator, the policy maker, the kingdom builder, whereas the business executive often can't pray for anything more than food, clothing, and physical security.

Many people think that God can't and won't do any more than take care of little matters! But his children know that there are far more important things that he wants to do; he only lacks a people of faith to lay hold of them. Faith enables a person to get above small matters (even though they are important, the Lord specifically told us that the Father will take care of them for us) and start dealing in miracles, the impossible, the big things of Heaven. Faith reaches for fire from Heaven. Faith lays hold of things that will build the kingdom of God on earth. Don't be content to pray for little matters anymore.

• ***Don't trust in yourself.*** If you really do have faith in God, you aren't going to rely any more on what you can do for yourself. Faith, by definition, sees that only God can do what you need. You need miracles, not self-help.

> Did you receive the Spirit by observing the Law, or by believing what you heard? Are you so foolish? After beginning with the Spirit, are you now trying to attain your goal by human effort? Have you suffered so much for nothing — if it really was for nothing? Does God give you his Spirit and work miracles among you because you observe the Law, or because you believe what you heard? (Galatians 3:2-5)

If you are praying for the kinds of things that you ought to be praying for, then you won't trust in yourself for anything. No man could ever do the works of God! What this world needs is a good dose of medicine from Heaven, not more of man's works. God calls us to labor with him in the world, and to obey him by doing such and such things, but he never said that those works of ours would actually change things for the better. They are only designed to set the stage, to clear the area, for the coming of God's power and wisdom. We are supposed to pick up and use the building blocks of Heaven when we work in this world: the righteousness of Christ, the wisdom of the Bible, the peace of the Holy Spirit, the love and acceptance of the Father, the strength and power of God, the plans and purposes of the Head of the Church, and so on. At each stage of the work we are prone to substitute our own materials for God's, but we have to resist the temptation. When you pray, ask for the things that last, the things that really make a difference in your life and in the lives of others. Get used to considering your own contribution as of no more value than any other servant's work.

• *Don't be deceived by appearances.* We often let appearances guide our prayers. Instead of praying for the impossible, for a miracle from God, we usually lower our sights and pray for something more reasonable. But appearances are always deceiving when we are dealing with spiritual matters.

> If you knew the gift of God and who it is
> that asks you for a drink, you would
> have asked him and he would have given
> you living water. (John 4:10)

Prayer is not an unimportant exercise; it's not a little ceremony that we do every day to keep God happy with us. Prayer is the opportunity of a lifetime! If the Spirit actually does bring you into God's presence during your prayer, that's the time to go for broke and stake everything on God's willingness to give. Don't waste the opportunity by asking for things that sound reasonable! In times past, when people were granted an audience with the king, they realized the tremendous importance of the occasion and they carefully prepared a request that would normally have seemed ridiculous and presumptuous. But on this once-in-a-lifetime opportunity they went for the best, the highest, something they couldn't get from lesser officials, because the king had consented to give them this one-time opportunity.

You are standing in front of someone who can do absolutely anything for you! Nothing is impossible for him. Don't let the petty little affairs of your life get you confused and backward-looking; don't look at the impossible situations in your life that call you back, in all reasonableness, away from God's throne. Here in front of God is the answer to all your problems, no matter how serious they are. Devils tremble when God's people pray! Rulers and powers and oppressors may succeed in putting you down for a while; but when you turn to God in prayer, they know the game is up for them — you are going to come back armed to the teeth with God's changing power.

Don't flub up by asking for little things; don't let appearances fool you. When you pray, you are coming to the One who can do anything that you need — and he is willing.

AN EXAMPLE PRAYER

It wasn't often that someone other than Jesus' immediate disciples called him "Lord" — but once a Gentile called him that! A Roman centurion, one of the hated ruling class, came to Jesus with a problem:

When Jesus had entered Capernaum, a centurion came to him, asking for help. "Lord," he said, "my servant lies at home paralyzed and in terrible suffering." Jesus said to him, "I will go and heal him." The centurion replied, "Lord, I do not deserve to have you come under my roof. But just say the word, and my servant will be healed. For I myself am a man under authority, with soldiers under me. I tell this one, 'Go,' and he goes; and that one, 'Come,' and he comes. I say to my servant, 'Do this,' and he does it." When Jesus heard this, he was astonished and said to those following him, "I tell you the truth, I have not found anyone in Israel with such great faith ... Go! It will be done just as you believed it would." (Matthew 8:5-10,13)

In the first place, the centurion could see that Jesus was a healer. He couldn't argue with that — the evidence was all around him. Actually it wasn't so much an act of faith for someone to come to Jesus for healing in those days, because he did so much of it and people could easily see him at it.

In the second place, we should notice that the centurion was crossing the dividing line between the Jews and the Romans. They just didn't mix with each other! The Romans were determined to keep the Jews under an iron fist, and the Jews hated the Romans' rule over them — they couldn't stand the thought that uncircumcised gentiles ruled their land. So this centurion was obviously desperate.

But he was more than desperate. He saw something in Jesus that was bigger than racial division. Let's study his prayer to see how his faith overcame human limitations:

- *He could see that Jesus was the Lord.* His faith enabled him to see past the deceiving mists of this world, deep into the world of God where the truth lives. It wasn't Jew and Roman any more, but the Lord of glory and the believer. The centurion knew that he was coming to God with his problem, not man. He knew that he *could* come to God in this way, that Jesus *would* listen to him because of his faith (and not get hung up about his position in society) and he knew that God *would* receive him as a believer — not as a Roman centurion. He also knew that the Pharisees were wrong about Jesus: this wasn't just a man, but the Son of God. He could see that Jesus was the person to talk to in order to get important things done.

- *He knew that Jesus' word was enough.* He got what he came for — the assurance that Jesus would heal his servant. The difference between the centurion and most everyone else, however, is that he believed in Christ's word. Most of us would have said to Jesus, "Yes, yes, but you must come now or it will be too late! " Not this man! When Jesus told him, "I will go and heal him," he immediately took confidence in Christ's word. He believed in Christ's miraculous power. We don't know how much of Jesus' ministry of miracles he was witness to, but that didn't matter in this case: his faith gave him complete confidence in Jesus' ability to fulfill his promise in whatever way he chose to do it — even in a way that, to all appearances, seemed impossible.

- *He considered the miracle as good as done.* He would have waited a million years and never given up. When Jesus said that he would heal his servant, the centurion completely trusted him. He wasn't worried about how it would happen or when it would happen because his faith showed him the heart of Christ. Jesus, he knew, would take care of him. He didn't go back home wondering and hoping that the Lord did something; he knew before he got home that the Lord heard him and answered him.

SUGGESTED PRACTICE

If you can pray in faith, you are already living by faith. Your prayers are just the natural results of your expectations. If you don't think that God will give you what he promised in his Word then you won't ask him for it; it's no use getting disappointed, is it! But if you expect that God is true to his Word, you will ask him for his promises — the full extent of those promises, no matter how impossible they sound — because nothing else will do. Your prayers will reflect the spiritual state of your heart.

There are some things that you can do to live the life of faith that he expects from you, and will result in prayers of faith:

- *Focus on what he said.* We already looked at the importance of using God's Word when you pray, and now we can press the point home. Study what he promised. Understand it fully. Be aware of how the world could never do such things, that man and men's systems can't fulfill their own promises, let alone do what God promises to do. Look at how the works of God are made out of the treasures of Heaven, not out of earthly things. There is so much you can learn from the Bible about what God does and how he does it, that your faith will inevitably grow as a result. Just as an informed citizen can help guide his country, an informed Christian will help build the kingdom of God.

• ***Search for testimony.*** If you have trouble believing that God really does some of the things the Bible says, then look for proofs. He doesn't mind; he recorded scores of miracles for the very purpose of proving that he does what he says. And you can find proofs of his promises in your own life and in the lives of people that you know. The Church is a place where we can swap stories about what God did for us; it greatly encourages each of us to see how the Lord worked in another person's circumstances.

• ***Don't ask for what you can do.*** Study how to avoid that problem. If what you ask for is something that man can do, you probably lack the faith to ask for what only God can do. Your world is too small; you don't see your problems in their true light; you overestimate the ability of your worldly pleasures to satisfy your soul. You need to start seeing the desperate predicament of the people around you, and the society that you live in. You need to admit that you need help and that you can't help yourself. You need to focus on the magnificence of God's inheritance for his saints — things that make the pleasures of this world look like worthless husks, or dung as Paul called it. You need to get a good view of God for a change; then you won't bother relying on anything or anybody else for what you need.

PRAY FOR HIS WILL

Your kingdom come, your will be done, on earth as it is in Heaven.
(Matthew 6:10)

When someone becomes a Christian, he stops living by his own will and starts living by God's instead. He used to live according to his own opinions and passions; whatever he wanted to do, that's what he did. But now he lives to please God: the things that he used to do, he can't do anymore; the things he once dreaded, now he looks forward to doing. It is perhaps this one aspect of Christianity that scares off unbelievers the most — they definitely do *not* want to change the way they live just to suit God's demands. They don't want to give up anything, least of all their own free will.

But new Christians take this thing of "the will of God" and run with it. Soon they are asking all sorts of questions: is my lifestyle acceptable to God? Do I think about the right things? Do I have the right friends? What can I do to help God's kingdom along? The biggest question of their lives becomes this: What is God's will for my life? And they spend a great deal of time searching for that answer — going to Bible studies, self-help conferences, counseling sessions, etc.

That's good in a way, but unfortunately they don't always seek God's will in every aspect of their lives. Prayer is one tragic and unexpected example. I have often seen people come to God as if he was Santa Claus; they produce long "Christmas lists" of requests that they want God to do for them! Instead of praying for God's will, they come to him with their own will! Instead of coming quietly to sit at God's feet and listen to what he has to say, they come to talk, and talk, and talk, without even considering that God may have something to say to them.

If people were much interested in God's will then they would pray in order to find it out, instead of praying their own thoughts and wishes out loud. Perhaps we need to get a better idea of who God really is — then we won't be so prone to steer the prayer session our own way.

A KING

When the Israelites finally came out of Egypt and slavery, they followed Moses to Mt. Sinai and there learned who this God was who delivered them from Pharaoh's hand. The Lord revealed his goodness, his love, the covenant and its terms, the laws that they must live by, the societal regulations for the nation, the military and economic structure that they were to have, and many other things. Above all, however, he revealed to them that he was their God, their King who had the right and the interest to rule the whole nation according to his own will. They learned that they must please him in every way, because he was their Master, their totalitarian ruler.

He proved to be a very strict ruler indeed. He governed their thoughts as well as their actions. He governed the small details of everyday life as well as the more important situations. He governed the little people as well as the powerful leaders. He demanded strict obedience, and dealt punishing blows when he didn't get it. He wasn't interested in excuses: everyone had to obey him, from the least to the greatest, and their works had to pass his strict inspection. Failures were destroyed.

We will admit that God was like this in the Old Testament, but we like to think that he changed in the New with the coming of Christ. But this view ignores the fact that the God whom Jesus showed us — the God of grace and love — is the God of the Old Testament too. We see God's love in the Old Testament, and his Law in the New. He doesn't change. Many people think that God softened his nature in Christ, that he eased up a good bit on his requirements. But that isn't true at all. He is still the King, the same exacting God who led the Israelites to the Incarnation of his Son. He was actually training his people in the Old Testament for the kind of life they should expect under the reign of the Messiah, the King of kings, in the New

Testament. If anything the expectations are tougher now! This is a prediction of what they could expect to find under the rule of Christ:

> Therefore, you kings, be wise; be warned, you rulers of the earth. Serve the LORD with fear and rejoice with trembling. Kiss the Son, lest he be angry and you be destroyed in your way, for his wrath can flare up in a moment. Blessed are all who take refuge in him. (Psalm 2:10-12)

For some reason Christians don't like to think of their gentle shepherd in this light. But when we call him Lord, we do it for good reason: our Jesus is, at this very minute, sitting in power over all the nations of the earth. He has their destinies in his hand. He is their Lord in the full sense of that word: a "despot" (as Peter calls him in 2 Peter 2:1, which is the Greek word behind the English translation of "Sovereign Lord") who *demands* their complete submission. And we call him Lord too — supposedly for the same reason.

Now modern Americans have a tough time with the idea of a king; we bought our personal freedoms at a great price and sacrifice, and we don't like to give them up to anybody — we are a very independent lot. But that is a dangerous attitude with God, toward whom we often have the same independent feelings. He is, whether we like it or not, and whether our culture "allows" it or not, the King. If you want a better idea of how exacting a Master he is, study the Sermon on the Mount; that's a King's proclamation of how he wants his kingdom to run.

We can characterize his kingship in these ways:

- *He has the right to rule.* "The LORD said to my Lord, 'Sit at my right hand until I make your enemies a footstool for your feet.'" (Psalm 110:1) God made us, and that gives him the right to decide our fate. We are here because he decided to put us here; we live on his planet, breathe his air, eat his food, look to him to protect us and lead us, and we use up his resources. And he will decide what to do with us — each one of us — whether we will be trophies of grace or "objects prepared for destruction." (Romans 9:22) "He determined the times set for them and the exact places where they should live." (Acts 17:26) And we can't really argue with him about any decision he makes about us, because he owns us body and soul; we are completely his to use as he chooses. "Does not the potter have the right to make out of the same lump of clay some pottery for noble purposes and some for common use?" (Romans 9:21)

• *He has profound insight.* "Does he who implanted the ear not hear? Does he who formed the eye not see? ... Does he who teaches man lack knowledge? The LORD knows the thoughts of man; he knows that they are futile." (Psalm 94:9) The Lord knows everything; it's his job to know, you might say, as Lord. We aren't going to surprise him with anything. On the contrary, it is we who are in the dark about things. We think we know so much, that we understand what we are doing and why our lives are the way they are; but God smiles at our childish arrogance. We actually know less about what is going on around us spiritually than a newborn infant knows of his surroundings. We only see this physical world (and very little of that!), whereas God sees the spiritual world as well — the towering realities that are pulling our hearts this way and that, the evil forces that are fighting and using every trick to lead us away from God's influence, the armies of angels overwhelming the earth to carry out God's continuing orders, the earth itself crying out under the burden of our sin, and so on and so on. He has a vast knowledge of the entire picture, compared to which our pitiful little insights are like a single grain of sand on the limitless shore of God's profound wisdom.

• *He has perfect plans.* "I make known the end from the beginning, from ancient times, what is still to come. I say: my purpose will stand, and I will do all that I please." (Isaiah 46:10) The Lord has his own ideas on what needs to be done and how it needs to be done.

The difference between his ideas and ours is this: his ideas work. They accomplish exactly what he wants from them. Our ideas always fall short of our expectations, and they certainly don't meet God's requirements. Oh, we have plenty of ideas; but either they don't measure up to God's moral standards, or they aren't realistic, or they will never work in the long run, or they don't take all the limitless details into consideration. What the Lord decides to do, however, is perfect because it draws upon and depends upon his vast wisdom and limitless power. His plans don't need any improvements from us; he isn't looking for any ideas from us, either.

• *He is utterly holy.* "Holy, holy, holy is the LORD Almighty; the whole earth is full of his glory." (Isaiah 6:3) The Lord is so staggeringly holy that he is like the picture of Sherman's army in its march across the South: God lays waste all the works of man as so much rebellion and vile sin; he scorches men's hearts and purges their immorality, like a blast furnace burning off the impurities; he forces people to bow their knees to him; he puts fear in peoples hearts at his approach. Angels tremble before God; men soon will, when the Lord comes in fire and wrath to judge their souls. He made this world and the people in it to be holy, and by his own Name he has sworn to make this planet fit for him and his people to live in for a change. He cannot and will not tolerate the least sin, the smallest bit of pride or arrogance or filth or immorality. Everything will be remade to his exacting (in some ways, terrifying) specifications. And he can smell the tiniest trace of sin even if it's covered over with the purest motives and the sweetest words. It isn't worthy of his consideration; it will never bring about the holy kingdom that he requires. That's why we have to be so careful when we pray.

• *He does good without fail.* "Every good and perfect gift is from above, coming down from the

Father of the Heavenly lights, who does not change like shifting shadows." (James 1:17) Jesus once compared the ability of men to give good things with God's ability: he said that there just isn't any fair comparison. "If you, then, though you are evil, know how to give good gifts to your children, how much more will your Father in Heaven give good gifts to those who ask him." (Matthew 7:11) Not only *can* he give good gifts, he *will* give them. We don't have to talk him into being nice and giving us things that we need; he loves his people more than we can imagine, and he has plans for an inheritance for them that staggers the human imagination. Furthermore, he knows *how* to give a good gift; we wrap up gifts in pretty paper and bows, but some of God's gifts come in plain wrapper and sometimes in a lot of pain and humiliation. Those kinds of gifts, though they may seem perplexing at first, turn out to be the most precious possessions that we have. "No discipline seems pleasant at the time, but painful. Later on, however, it produces a harvest of righteousness and peace for those who have been trained by it." (Hebrews 12:11) The Lord knows how to bless us in any and every situation that we live through; what is one man's curse is another man's Heaven.

- *He rules by unerring justice.* "For the LORD is righteous, he loves justice; upright men will see his face." (Psalm 11:7) Whenever we get the raw end of someone's dirty dealing, we will often go to God for "justice." But if we could see how *just* God really is, we might think twice about demanding justice. He sees exactly what is in each person's heart, missing no detail no matter how small, and he deals with each of us according to a fairness that is scary. He judges by his Law, an exact and extremely complex system that only he knows how to apply. Since he does things for his own glory and according to his own will, he judges our thoughts and actions according to the Law without any regard to who we are or whether we think we should be exempt from his impossibly high standards. "For it is time for judgment to begin with the family of God; and if it begins with us, what will the outcome be for those who do not obey the gospel of God?" (1 Peter 4:17) The one who comes to God with a problem against his brother may find God pointing back at him, at the log of sin in his own eye. (Matthew 7:3-5)

This is the kind of King we have over us. The point ought to be pretty plain to us: he knows exactly what he is doing. He doesn't need anybody to counsel him. "Who has known the mind of the Lord? Or who has been his counselor?" (Romans 11:34) We can't improve on his plans, nor do we have details that he isn't aware of already, nor does he need our guidance as to what is the right and holy thing to do. Just to think that makes one laugh, really; only someone who doesn't have the faintest notion of who the Lord is can think that he can help the Lord in any way with advice and opinions.

Does this bother you? Are you perhaps a little offended at the idea that God doesn't need you? Good — you are getting a clearer idea of who this God is that you come to in prayer. He isn't a flat image on the wall, a lifeless doll on a crucifix — he isn't someone that we can control. He controls us! If we make the mistake of rushing into God's presence with a lot on our minds that we want him to take care of, we may find ourselves (if the Spirit is gracious and opens our eyes to his majesty) falling on our faces in fear instead. Israel trembled when God came down on Mt. Sinai. Isaiah cried out anguish at the sight of God — God brought the topic of discussion to the table and the prophet was afraid of what God would say to him. The disciples shook in fear in Jesus' presence when he calmed the storm – they hadn't known that he was someone to fear. It changed their relationship with him considerably.

OUR WILLFULNESS

If there is one characteristic that we can use to describe a sinner, it is this: he does what he wants instead of what God wants. John defines sin in this way: "Sin is lawlessness." (1 John 3:4) When we don't do exactly what God says to do, for whatever reason, then we aren't living according to God's will.

It may be argued that nobody can do exactly what God requires. That's true, in a way, but the fact remains that we can't do it because of our sin — we are guilty just because we *don't want* to obey God, not because we *can't*. God would never threaten people with everlasting Hell for doing something they couldn't help! God punishes deliberate sinners, not the righteous. On the other hand, you underestimate man's deep-seated hatred of God's rule over him if you think that there are people who submit willingly without God having something drastic done first to change their souls. We are all born into sin, into willfulness, into rebellion, in some way or another, to some degree.

Willfulness is deeply ingrained into our hearts. We don't like these kingly characteristics of God. He may interfere too much with our lives. If we accepted the fact that God demands such complete control over us, we would have to give up things that are precious to us. And we aren't going to do that willingly. At the very least we are going to find a way to please God and please ourselves at the same time; we have clever tricks to make it appear that such an impossible thing will work. At the very worst, there are a lot of people who don't care at all about God being King — they are their own masters and they are proud of it.

When God demands something from us, these are the things that go on in our hearts:

- **We argue against it.** We will always come up with a dozen "good" reasons why we can't do things God's way. It isn't reasonable, it doesn't make good sense; nobody else is doing it; I don't have time now; God is different nowadays — he doesn't expect us to do that in the twentieth century; I would look like a fool if I did that; that's just plain wrong; our experts disagree; and so on.

- **We ignore it.** Either we don't read that part of the Bible, or we avoid teaching and preaching it; we don't give it any serious thought; we don't bring it up for discussion in church or conferences; we don't pray about it; we hope that God will forget about it too if we just assume that it isn't part of our modern faith.

• **We reinterpret it.** Instead of taking the Word of God in its plain words, we come up with all sorts of versions that suit us better. Words mean different things nowadays, we say; what God really means here is ...; if we want to apply it to our own context, it must mean something different; I really think that, if Jesus were here now, he would put it in an entirely different way. It's just too easy to put a new meaning — *our* meaning — on words that offend us as they stand; God doesn't strike us with lightning when we do, and that makes us bolder.

• **We dilute it down.** Instead of accepting the sharpness of God's scalpel, we blunt the edge a good bit so that it doesn't hurt us. We continue to use the Name of the Lord but it is stripped of its power; we praise God for his attributes but we don't believe half of what those attributes teach us about him. We cut the living flesh of Christianity to the bone, leaving only a few ragged pieces of skin here and there, ending up with a religion named after Christ but with very little resemblance to the one he formed in the beginning.

• **We shift the emphasis over to our own glory.** If we simply *have* to do God's will, then we are going to try to make it look as if we *approved* of his plan — not that we submitted to him. We will say, in effect, "I thought of this great idea and God promised to bless me in it!" As if the world will thank God that such resourceful and determined Christians are busy doing good deeds for everyone! What would God do without us?

The end result is that we are so used to leaning away from God's will, and doing things the way we want, that praying isn't going to change any of that. We can say that we are seeking God's will, but before it is all over, the will of God is going to get twisted and turned into something that suits our will instead. We have subtle ways of doing this; in fact, we probably aren't even aware of the fact that we do it. But you really can't expect much better from someone who has thought of himself for so long and of God's will so little. Habits die hard — especially habits that make us feel like we are in control.

THE PURPOSE OF PRAYER

There's a saying about prayer that has been around for a long time, which is this: "Prayer changes things." With all due respect to good men in the past who have filled that saying with precious meaning, I'd like to alter it a bit and give it a different emphasis. It really should read like this instead:

The purpose of prayer is to change YOU.

First of all, *something* needs changing. We don't pray just to pass the time; prayer isn't a ceremonial occasion in which we talk about nothing in particular. We pray when there is a crisis, a real need, when something needs to be done that only God can do. If it were any less serious then we wouldn't need to pray about it!

Second, the Lord doesn't need to change. If he is as much of a king as we saw above, then we shouldn't be surprised, when we come to him in prayer, to find him already in control of things. He is way ahead of us.

- *You aren't going to tell God anything new.* He knows the end from the beginning. He knows what will happen and everything about what has already happened. He knows what you are thinking, and he knows what everyone else who is concerned is thinking. You aren't going to tell him anything that he doesn't already know. In fact, he may just let *you* in on more of the details than you were aware of! It's you who aren't aware of the whole story yet. Too often we run off to tell God that we need something, when he already knows that and he has already made provisions for us: "Your Heavenly Father knows that you need them." (Matthew 6:32)

• *He already knows what he is going to do.* You don't have to tell him what to do; he doesn't need your help to figure things out. That's like a child telling his father where to turn when they are driving home. It's cute, but the grownups don't need the child's advice. We can't possibly figure things out well enough to know what God must do in order to solve the situation; there are simply too many variables, it's too complex for our finite minds. Whatever solution we would come up with wouldn't solve the problem anyway. Besides, too often our sinful hearts fall in love with a solution that will let us continue in our sin; he can't afford to give us what may lead us into sin. We've lived long enough working out our own problems, and what have we got to show for it? Not salvation! It's God's turn now to use *his* solutions: step aside.

• *He wants to see you in-step with his plans.* It's you who have to be filled in on the details. It's you who have to change your ways, not the Lord. He has a very precise, very precious, very powerful answer for your problems; what he wants to see in you is some real interest in his solution. He hears so many prayers from people who have no interest or desire at all for what he offers us in Christ; but when we actually ask for what he has given us in Christ, that gets his immediate attention. When we want his deliverance (his style, his way) then he gets his armies together and charges at our enemies. When we want food from Heaven (which he has prepared for us in Christ) then he stokes the ovens and showers it down on us. In other words, God sets his plans into motion when we come and submit to everything that he wants to do.

Keep in mind the Lord's overall plan. He wants primarily to establish his kingdom on earth — in every corner, in every man's mind, in every action and thought, in every situation. He only needs a willing people to get it started. The kind of people he wants is men and women who completely put aside their own will and open themselves to his will. They don't want to introduce their own ideas because they know that their ideas and desires lead to death; we have plenty of proof for that. What they want for a change is what God does — which is life and health, "righteousness, peace, and joy in the Holy Spirit." (Romans 14:17) It will be a world in which God alone decides what is best for man, and man trusts God completely to make those decisions for him.

Then what is prayer? Prayer is simply telling God that you aren't your own person anymore. You are saying to him, "Lord, your Word, what you promised, this is what I want. This is my problem, this is my need, but I don't even trust myself to understand that as you do. And your answer is (*fill in the blank*); this is what you want for my life. 1 submit to your will; I put my own wishes away — crucify the willfulness and rebellion against your kingdom in my heart — and I ask you to do what you want to do in me."

Now this appears to present some difficulties. If the Lord is going to do something anyway, why pray about it? And if we didn't pray about something, would God go ahead and do what he had planned, even though we aren't in step with him? But that's exactly the point! It seems like an innocent question, but really it's not: we aren't supposed to be wondering what God will do if we sin! As a matter of fact the Lord will do exactly what he wants whether or not we are in step with him; but what he *would* have done (as opposed to what he ended up doing) if we had acted differently isn't our business. Our business is to obey him, to seek his will and do it. If we do that then we can expect God to act according to his promises; if we don't, then he will still do his own will, but it may or may not be what we wanted or expected. He takes his own counsel.

To the faithful you show yourself faithful, to the blameless you show yourself blameless, to the pure you show yourself pure, but to the crooked you show yourself shrewd. (Psalm 18:25-26)

WHAT IS GOD'S WILL?

If we are to pray for God's will, then what is his will? What should we be asking for? The answer to that important question is ... only God knows! It's a serious mistake for someone to tell someone else what the will of God is for their lives, except in very general terms. We can know generally what God expects from others, but only their Lord knows what that person must do, in any given situation, to please him. It's a very personal affair.

But since his will is in his Word (we won't find it anywhere else) we can categorize the kinds of things that God expects from us. Some of the headings would be:

> • *He wants to save you from sin and death.* "He is patient with you, not wanting anyone to perish, but everyone to come to repentance." (2 Peter 3:9) The most important thing that God wants to do for you is to save you. So it would help matters greatly if you fall in line with his program for your life. He is going to sanctify you one way or another: either you will learn to walk in his ways willingly or he will bring you through trials and setbacks and hurts so that you will submit to his will. Don't be surprised that, for this greatest of all his works, he has a lot of ways to accomplish it; and whenever you pray, he is going to bring the subject up again and again.

> You can't very well avoid being saved when he is so determined to do it to you. He *wants* to judge men's hearts. "The Word of God ... judges the thoughts and attitudes of the heart. Nothing in all creation is hidden from God's sight. Everything is uncovered and laid bare before the eyes of him to whom we must give an account." (Hebrews 4:12-13)

> If there is one thing about man that constantly needs doing, it's uncovering his heart. We always have so much hidden there — things that we are hiding from each other and things that we try to hide from God.

And because we hide our sins and ugly places, we manage to fool others into thinking that we are better, stronger, smarter, nicer, and more desirable than we really are. But God doesn't sit still for such deceit, not from even the best of us. We all hide a deep well of wickedness in our hearts; there is enough sin and ignorance inside us to ruin the world. So the first thing he is going to do, when we come into his presence, is to strip us bare. The only covering that he will allow us is the righteousness of Christ, not our own attempts at clothing ourselves with our false works and deceitful goodness. He wants to strip away our "fig leaf" solutions and get at the problem, not let us continue to hide it from him.

• *He wants to honor his Name.* "Let him who walks in the dark, who has no light, trust in the Name of the LORD and rely on his God." (Isaiah 50:10) There is a lot of power and possibility in the Name of God, as we have seen already. There is a good reason for that – it's a resource for God's people to draw upon. The Lord wants us to learn his many names, to find out what they teach us about him, to call upon God by those names, and to trust him for what those names describe about him. As we begin doing that we will find that he is true to his Name, which will make us all the more willing to turn to him the next time we need that kind of help. And others will see us getting such a rich feast from God in this way; they will see that he is the only one to turn to for help. All this brings him glory, which he deserves; and you will find, when you pray to him, that he expects you to pick up on all this.

• *He wants to build a Kingdom.* "Then the end will come, when he hands over the kingdom to God the Father after he has destroyed all dominion, authority and power." (1 Corinthians 15:24) This is always uppermost on God's agenda and you will find it to be true when you pray — if the Spirit really does bring you to God when you pray. He expects you to bow your knee before him. Whether you do it physically or not isn't the point; there are many, many people who pray on their knees, in a show of reverence, who have no intention of obeying the will of God in their hearts and lives. He wants absolute, total submission, as a slave gives his master, as a child gives his father. He wants a world in which the only thing that is ever done is what he wants. He wants man's will to turn around and agree with him 100%; any deviation from his will must be totally destroyed. In other words, you will find, when you pray, that he won't listen to what you want unless you change your will to fit in with what he wants.

Now, you can work out the details for these and other general topics that are discussed in the Bible; what they might look like in your own life may be different from the experiences of other people. But from these general subjects you will very quickly get into personal applications — that is, what God wants *you* to do. You may not know exactly what his will is for you in a particular circumstance, but your confusion shouldn't last for long; armed with the Scripture, and the Spirit bringing you into God's presence, he will make his will very plain to you. This business of ruling the world is important to him; when you submit to him, he will not fail to rule you. Your obedience is a golden opportunity for him.

PRAYING FOR HIS WILL

Since it is we who need changing during prayer, not God, then our prayers should take on a different look than when we used to pray for our own wishes. Instead of hauling out our "Christmas lists" and demanding things from the Lord, we should expect God to demand things from us. Prayer is coming to get our orders from God, not giving him orders!

- *Crisis praying.* Perhaps it will be easier to think in terms of God's will if we look at the times we need to pray. Prayer is for when no human help can solve a problem, and yet the problem must be solved. We are in a crisis: if we don't get help then disastrous things are going to happen. Prayer is when we pull out the big guns of our spiritual war; we have to get something from God this time.

> My loved one had a vineyard on a fertile hillside. He dug it up and cleared it of stones and planted it with the choicest vines. He built a watchtower in it and cut out a wine press as well. Then he looked for a crop of good grapes, but it yielded only bad fruit. (Isaiah 5:1-2)

Life for God's children is a wine press. He plants the seeds in our hearts for faith and love and hope, and he waters it with the ministry of men, and he expects good fruit to come out of our hearts – the fruit of the Spirit: love, joy, peace, patience, kindness, goodness, faithfulness, gentleness and self-control. (Galatians 5:22-23) And what squeezes us? The crises in life! The problems and trials, the nasty neighbor across the fence, the troubles, the disasters, the personal failures when we sin against our Father. When things like these happen (and life consists of them to a large degree) the Lord wants to see if the good seed that he planted in our hearts will result in spiritual fruit. He would never expect spiritual goodness from a person who didn't have the Spirit in him.

There is nothing that isn't a spiritual issue in our lives. Everything is either black or white; either we obey God or we don't; either we trust him for what we need, or we rely on ourselves or other gods; either we honor him with our actions and words or we dishonor him. Even the simplest matters are really spiritual concerns: the food we eat, the clothes we wear — do we run after them like pagans or do we trust our Father who knows we need them? (Matthew 6:31-33)

So when you have a problem or an issue to pray about, you are really at a spiritual crossroads: you have the choice of either getting God's answer, which will glorify him and humble you, or of looking for an answer that is not God's will and so bring dishonor on God and shame on yourself. The issues of your life are more important to God than you may think; more hangs in the balance than you may realize. You can't afford to make the smallest slip when you pray — you must find God's will or your life will start collapsing, just a little at first but later in huge chunks, like the house built on sand. Remember the old saying: for want of a nail the war was lost!

• *Find out what his will is.* In order to do this you must become familiar with the book where his will is recorded. Some people think that God's will drops out of the sky painted in big red letters, and until they see that they aren't going to change their ways. But God already told us what he wants us to do, and he isn't going to change his mind about it. The details of how you must do his will – those will be peculiar to your own situation; but the principles are in the Bible already.

Let God set the agenda for your prayers. Don't bring your own lists, things that you think are important, things that you feel *must* be dealt with. Even though they may sound good, they are probably just enough different from the way that God sees it that he will insist on creating his own agenda. "In his heart a man plans his course, but the LORD determines his steps." (Proverbs 16:9)

There are many times when we come to God in prayer not knowing what his will is for us, even after studying the Bible. There's nothing wrong with that. But don't therefore run off and make up your own answers! Think about the kind of problem you have; as we have said, it is a spiritual crisis in which you are supposed to be doing God's will or your own will. Somewhere in the Bible it talks about a situation like that; find it and study how the people who were involved acted. Look at their faith — or their unbelief. Watch God as he dealt with them; look for his righteous judgment of their hearts. Bring all this to God, along with your own situation, and ask him for wisdom. James says that a faith like this will move God to answer with just the solution that you need. (James 1:5-6) You will inevitably find that, although God's will for you is specially fitted to your case, you had the answer all along in the Word that you read. You just needed the Spirit to open your eyes to see it.

• *Get ready to change.* Remember that God's ways are not our ways. Not only does God's will offend us at times (and we come up with all sorts of reasons why we don't want to take it seriously) but many times it isn't at all what we would have expected him to say. The rich young ruler thought he had eternal life in the bag when he asked Jesus, "What must I do to inherit eternal life?" (Mark 10:17-22) Christ's will took him completely off-guard; he walked away from the Lord disappointed and not at all ready to obey him.

This is going to happen more than you realize. There is a lot of rebellion and self-will in your heart, for one thing, and there is much to change in your life, for another. When God keeps telling you that this and this and this have got to change if you want to please him, he's going to hit a raw nerve somewhere. We all seem to have a believing point beyond which we are not willing to go; we may believe a lot or a little of God's Word, but somewhere there is the straw that we can't accept — it's just too much to expect from us. *That's* what you have to work on; crucify yourself and your will and submit to God's will and you will be saved.

• *Submit to him.* All God's children are also his servants. We may be unworthy servants, but he expects service out of us nonetheless. He may be our Father, but he is also our Lord. Don't let one of his names mislead you into thinking that his other names don't mean anything. There are severe penalties threatened to those who presume on God's love and don't obey him in all things. It will be those who persevere to the end who will be saved. (Matthew 10:22) Those who used his Name in worship and "service" but never came to him and consulted his will, they will be thrust out of the kingdom. (Matthew 7:21-23) He demands faith first, obedience second, then the rest of the graces. "But the man who looks intently into the perfect law that gives freedom, and continues to do this, not forgetting what he has heard, but doing it — he will be blessed in what he does." (James 1:25)

AN EXAMPLE PRAYER

There is probably no better example in Scripture of praying for God's will than the Lord Jesus Christ's own prayer before he was crucified. The struggle he went through during this prayer, none of us can even imagine: he was God's only Son, about to be cut off from his Father (a seemingly unthinkable situation), headed for the wrath that God's judgment inflicts on sinners, and carrying all the sin of multitudes of sinners upon his heart — while still remaining sinless himself during the entire crisis. When he came to Gethsemane, this is what happened:

They went to a place called Gethsemane, and Jesus said to his disciples, "Sit here while I pray." He took Peter, James and John along with him, and he began to be deeply distressed and troubled. "My soul is overwhelmed with sorrow to the point of death," he said to them. "Stay here and keep watch." Going a little farther, he fell to the ground and prayed that if possible the hour might pass from him. "Abba, Father," he said, "everything is possible for you. Take this cup from me. Yet not what I will, but what you will." (Mark 14:32-36)

You should note these things about the Lord's prayer:

- *As a man, he had his own wishes.* Now whatever the Lord Jesus could have wanted would never have been sinful; he only wanted righteousness, goodness, the glory of God. It was impossible for him to want anything that was wrong. And at this point his body and soul were screaming out in spiritual holy protest at the coming crucifixion. The author of life should never have to experience death — and a shameful death at that! The Son should never have to be separated from the Father! The Holy One of Israel didn't have to take the sins of his people on himself! The whole affair was unthinkable! It probably had the angels amazed. This is the grief that Jesus was experiencing on the verge of his death. When we get in tough situations we also struggle with our own feelings; but we can't trust ourselves to look at the problem in a pure, holy, righteous, and just way. Jesus, however, certainty could and did; and that's what he came to the Father bearing in his heart.

- *He prayed for the Father's will in this crisis.* But he willingly set aside his own will — as pure and right as that may have been, in his case — and asked for the Father's will instead. Notice what he struggled with here: it wasn't that he was for life and the Father was for death; they weren't working for opposite goals. He didn't stumble over the fact that he was being asked to do something unfair. In submitting to the Father's will he wasn't reluctantly accepting death; he was accepting whatever the Father would choose to do with him. For all he knew, the Father just may "take the cup" away from him and give him life. "Everything is possible for you." What he was submitting to was God's *control*, not any specific decision. He turned away from the pain of what he had to do, so that he could obey his Father and honor him with that submission. *Whatever* the Father chose to do with him, he was ready to submit to it. As a matter of fact he knew very well what the Father had sent him to do; he previously gave his disciples several warnings about his approaching death, and even taught them what it would mean for men's souls. Here, when it had come to the point of going through with it, even though the idea was against all reasonable arguments to the contrary, he gave up his own will and put himself under the will of God.

• *He learned obedience.* He changed. We have to be careful about how we apply that idea to the "One who never changes," however. His nature didn't change, his work didn't change, his goals didn't change, and his methodology didn't change; but he changed his own will to conform to the Father's will. He always did claim to do only the Father's will; he was used to *putting his own will aside*, no matter how holy it was, in order to do God's will. "When you have lifted up the Son of Man, then you will know who I am and that I do nothing on my own but speak just what the Father has taught me." (John 8:28) "My food is to do the will of him who sent me and to finish his work." (John 4:34) And in this last crisis of his life he did it one more time.

> During the days of Jesus' life on earth, he offered up prayers and petitions with loud cries and tears to the one who could save him from death, and he was heard because of his reverent submission. Although he was a son, he learned obedience from what he suffered and, once made perfect, he became the source of eternal salvation for all who obey him. (Hebrews 5:7-9)

He purposely put aside what his own body and soul wanted – we can see him do that in this passage — and submitted himself to whatever God the Father wanted. He had enough faith in his Father to realize that whatever God wanted, would be good and proper and exactly what would glorify him the most. He prayed in order to conform himself to his Father's will.

SUGGESTED PRACTICE

Probably the best advice in the Bible along these lines can be found in the book of Ecclesiastes:

> Guard your steps when you go to the house of God. Go near to listen rather than to offer the sacrifice of fools, who do not know that they do wrong. Do not be quick with your mouth, do not be hasty in your heart to utter anything before God. God is in Heaven and you are on earth, so let your words be few. As a dream comes when there are many cares, so the speech of a fool when there are many words ... Therefore stand in awe of God. (Ecclesiastes 5:1-3,7)

There is a lot of wisdom in this passage, practical points that we should keep in mind when we pray — especially when we want to know God's will.

First, don't go into prayer ready to run your mouth. Keep quiet a while and look at God first. Worship him; fear him; get him in view, through the Spirit, in the Word that reveals him, so that you know you are there with him. A little spiritual quiet will act like a focusing lens on the realities of Heaven. Our earthly cares tend to fog the image of Heaven and make us doubt that we are really there.

Second, listen to God. He speaks through his Word; he guides with his Spirit; he uses his servants (he has many servants, some human and some not) to work his will on you. He has much to say to you; you are the learner, he is the Teacher; you are the child, he is the Father. Don't think that prayer is a one-way communication, and don't get the idea that you are the principal speaker. Everyone is waiting to see what God says, not what you say.

Third, realize that your understanding of your situation probably isn't complete — it may even be wrong. God has an excellent vantage point in Heaven where he can see much more than you can; you are on earth, in your little context, and you don't even know the depths of your own heart. After he enlightens you about the real situation and state of things, you may come away from prayer with a different point of view.

Fourth, be careful about your problems and how you bring them to the Lord. Sure, you hurt under burdens and trials, and these things do worry you. But when you let loose at God with all these cares, you may sometimes say things that show how little faith you really have. You may say things that dishonor the Name of the one who has been taking care of you all along. How can a well-fed, well-taught, protected Christian, who has the treasures of Heaven to look forward to, and the Spirit in his heart to overcome sin and death, and forgiveness of all his sins, say that nothing ever goes right in life?! If that's the way you pray, God isn't going to feel a bit sorry for you; he will harden and consider your "prayer" as a "speech of a fool." You're not going to get any answers until your attitude changes.

Above all, keep in mind that prayer is a time for finding out God's will and getting in line with it. He will tell you his will if you are willing to set yours aside.

PRAY FOR HIS GLORY

For from him and through him and to him are all things. To him be the glory forever! Amen. (Romans 11:36)

Life is a busy stage, as Shakespeare once wrote, with men and women flitting across the world for their brief appearance and then forever disappearing. Some of them manage to get lots of attention — because of their dress, their customs, their political or economic or military achievements — but most of humanity slides by the inspection of history virtually unnoticed by later generations. "Generations come and generations go, but the earth remains forever ... There is no remembrance of men of old, and even those who are yet to come will not be remembered by those who follow." (Ecclesiastes 1:4,11)

It is this anonymity, the possibility of not being noticed by anybody, that most bothers each one of us. From the time we are children, on through our teenage years, and into our productive adult lives, we struggle to be noticed. We want to make our mark on the world; we vow that someone after us will remember us, somehow. We want to be looked up to and respected; we want people to need us; we want children to carry our names and characteristics and memories. In fact, we invent ways to draw attention to ourselves. When we die, we leave stone markers with our names on them in a last-ditch attempt to force the world to take notice of us.

While we are so busy trying to carve our names on the trees of life, we hardly ever notice that God seems to be missing. We are so self-centered by nature that, when there is applause and approval of men, we take all the credit for ourselves – even though the Lord may have been the real hero. We get the applause, the jobs, the church positions, the places of power and decision. We get the blessings, the attention of men, the successes. We feel good when we are needed, and terrible when everyone rejects us — as if they can't afford to reject us. But where is God?

When we pray, we again tend to center on ourselves. "Lord, make me this way, and make me like that, and give me this thing that I need, and take this sin out of me, and give me the ability to do such and such" — our prayers, as any language expert can testify, are about us. But where is God?

Now in one sense that is understandable, because the reason for prayer is to deal with issues in our lives; we need God's help to solve our problems. But in another sense it is completely wrong. It's as if we are only using God as a resource up there in Heaven, and the real work is happening down here on earth and we are the heroes. "Just checking in, Lord — if you wouldn't mind dropping some grace down the chute, I'll take it from there." God stays in Heaven, in other words, like a story, a grandfather image, someone we go to when we pray but who remains in that "other" world while we come back alone to face our life's challenges. Sometimes we will ask that he walk with us, as he promised us, but we don't expect anybody else (especially unbelievers) to see him when he does. He is only real to us in our minds, through our "faith."

It's no wonder then that we pray about ourselves so much of the time. If God really does stay up there in Heaven, and here we are facing the world on our own, then prayer is only a matter of transferring accounts — moving some spiritual treasures from God's account in Heaven to our account here on earth. It's still up to us to do something with it because, basically, we are standing alone. It seems that we believe that God only acts long distance, by proxy, by sending *us* in his Name to do all the work.

The problem with that kind of thinking is that God doesn't like it at all. While we pray to him, asking him for spiritual resources and grace and forgiveness and guidance so that we can do something with it, he impatiently wonders why we don't ask *the big question*. In fact, don't expect him to answer any of your prayers until you ask him for what he's been waiting for a long time for you to ask him — for his glory.

WHAT IS GLORY?

The Hebrew word for "glory" is *kabod*, and it comes from the verb "to be heavy" or "to be honored." The word was often used to describe gold — which is both heavy and precious. It conjures up images of kings sitting in massive golden thrones, robed in rich crimson and velvet, covered with jewels, wearing a golden crown and holding a gem studded scepter, surrounded by ministers of state and the wealth and power of the kingdom. As a matter of fact, this was the word used when the Israelites talked about such kings — glory that was heavy with wealth and importance and majesty.

It is used most often, however, in respect to God. We know that the Lord has infinite wealth, that his throne is "heavy" in a way that earthly thrones can't match, that somehow his glory is far greater than anything we find on earth. But the Lord's glory is different than gold and jewels; whereas we adorn a man with these marks of wealth which makes him glorious, the Lord is already glorious without them. He is glorious without any earthly adornment:

> The Word became flesh and lived for a while among us.
> We have seen his glory, the glory of the one and only
> Son, who came from the Father, full of grace and truth.
> (John 1:14)

It's probably the case that when man adorns himself with riches in order to look "glorious" he is actually trying to imitate God's natural glory, the look of power and wealth. But even if a man is covered with these things outwardly, it remains to be seen if he really does have power; there have been many kings who have looked the part but haven't been able to produce. Take the present "kingdom" of England, for example: the man or woman who sits on the throne certainly has the appearance of ruling the nation, but as a matter of fact it's all show — they have no power at all, and their wealth is provided by the people for nostalgia's sake.

But God is a different matter. His glory is of such a nature that, if we would see it, we would be immediately convinced that here is the real thing. When we speak of glory in respect to God, we mean two things:

• *He gets the credit.* There's a lot that goes on in the world that man takes credit for, but we may be surprised at who is really responsible for it all. This is God's world in a more profound sense than any of us know. He came up with its design, from the smallest and least significant structure to the largest and most complex structures — and he wove all the relationships of the parts together into a living world. Man only reshapes the materials that God first made. Man borrows ideas from God's infinite creativity and ingenuity.

"Credit" means who actually did something, who is responsible for it. We all love to take the credit for doing helpful things — and when things go wrong, none of us want to take the blame for it. We give credit by handing out rewards (or punishments) and honor to the appropriate people: we give trophies and awards, we erect memorials, we write books about them, we give raises or high grades to them, and so on.

But when we give someone credit for something that they didn't do, something's gone very wrong. In the first place, they weren't responsible for doing this thing and they ought not to be claiming the credit for it — that's dishonest. In the second place, we are looking to the wrong person and giving praise to an impostor, when the real hero goes completely unnoticed.

As a matter of fact, that's exactly the case with God. He is responsible for so much in our lives that we ought to be giving him the credit for virtually everything we have; but either we have forgotten him, or we grow tired of giving him all the credit, or we want some of the credit ourselves — in any case the Lord often gets no credit for things. We don't read about him in the newspapers, though he directs the affairs of men. We don't read about him in textbooks, though he designed and created the entire world that we study, including man's mind itself. We don't see him mentioned in any political platform, even though his Law is perfect and pure and capable of judging nations. We can look anywhere and see almost no reference to God, even though he is behind everything.

He gave us the air we breathe and the food we eat: "The eyes of all look to you, and you give them their food at the proper time." (Psalm 145:15) The Lord made the world in all its richness and usefulness and gave it to men to use: "With my great power and outstretched arm I made the earth and its people and the animals that are on it, and I give it to anyone I please." (Jeremiah 27:5) The Lord decides where and when all of us will live: "From one man he made every nation of men, that they should inhabit the whole earth; and he determined the times set for them and the exact places where they should live." (Acts 17:26) It's the Lord who opens the eyes of the soul and gives spiritual life: "But because of his great love for us, God, who is rich in mercy, made us alive with Christ even when we were dead in transgressions — it is by grace you have been saved." (Ephesians 2:5) We have no hope of ever being holy and righteous unless the Lord makes us righteous: "And I will put my Spirit in you and move you to follow my decrees and be careful to keep my laws." (Ezekiel 36:27) The Lord alone will fight our battles: "The LORD will fight for you; you need only to be still." (Exodus 14:14) If we are going to get into Heaven, God is going to have to do it for us — we cannot: "For my Father's will is that everyone who looks to the Son and believes in him shall have eternal life, and I will raise him up at the last day." (John 6:40)

In fact, you will find that God has something to do with just about everything in your life. It's like a luxury liner: guests may think that food and drink appear out of nowhere, and everything is fun and excitement, and the captain is a model of courtesy and a wonderful dinner companion. What they don't see, however, unless they start exploring the ship and going into doors marked "For Personnel Only," are the many hundreds of crew making the voyage possible — it takes around-the-clock vigilance to keep the ship safe, well-stocked, and moving! In the same way, people don't realize how much God is involved in their lives — if it weren't for his constant vigilance, his never-ending supplies, his protective hand, and his unearthly power and wisdom forcing the earth to conform to his will, we would have all been dead long ago.

But God doesn't get the credit for the smallest part of all this. We act as if everything in life just happens on its own. We say that science is the one giving us a good life, or it's due to the power and wealth of the country we live in. We even take the credit for things ourselves — *we* build peace on earth, *we* solve political problems, *we* feed the hungry, *we* educate people and make them useful, *we* build God's kingdom in the Church.

In the meantime, where is God? Who is talking about him? You've probably seen the comedy line where one of the pair keeps putting himself in front of the camera and cutting the other one out – he answers all the questions and does all the talking, even though you know he doesn't know what he's talking about. It's the same way here, with God and man: we keep putting ourselves in the limelight and keep trying to steal the show, as if it's us that everyone wants to see and God has a small, if any, part in what is going on.

• ***The greatness of his presence.*** The Lord's presence is a different kind of thing than we are used to. Man's greatness often puts us in awe: we will fall all over our feet when we find ourselves in the presence of important men and women, for example our elected officials. But even the greatest of men is still a human being, and a sinner at that; as the saying goes, he has to put his pants on in the morning just as we do. The

Lord, however, is Spirit — not created like us — and he makes his presence known in a way that staggers us in awe and fear.

Take the example of Jesus in the Garden of Gethsemane. When the soldiers followed Judas up the path to their victim, Jesus met them with these words: "I am he." (John 18:6) The soldiers, the text says, drew back and fell to the ground. It's as if those words were a revelation to these men of who Jesus really was; they came to arrest him, but he arrested them instead! Suddenly he wasn't just an ordinary man — he was God, emanating a power that threw them back as if before a Master. I have a feeling that *he* led *them* back down the path to his execution!

Or how about the time when Solomon finished building the Temple in Jerusalem — the magnificent structure that replaced the old Tabernacle that Moses had made hundreds of years before. Solomon didn't spare any expense in making the Temple one of the most glorious buildings in the Middle East. Yet that glory of gold and silver and ornate carvings, though awe-inspiring to see, didn't give the Israelites even the tiniest notion of what it would be like when God moved in to live there:

> Then the Temple of the LORD was filled with a cloud, and the priests could not perform their service because of the cloud, for the glory of the LORD filled the Temple of God. (2 Chronicles 5:13-14)

They talked about God, and they designed the Temple with God's service in mind, and they surely thought that they knew God; but when he came, it was an experience that they could never have predicted and they never forgot. He crushed them with his presence; they moved out of his way in fear and awe as he took possession of his house. They could no more come close to him than the Israelites could when God stepped down onto Mt. Sinai and shook the earth with his fearful presence.

When God comes close to earth, strange things happen. When the Maker of all things comes to visit his world, mountains leap for joy and trees clap their hands. Storming seas become calm; Mt. Sinai, we read, smoked, and thunder and lightning leapt around its summit. The Red Sea split apart under his hand. The dead get up and walk out of their tombs. We think that there are set laws that the universe runs by; but when God approaches, all those laws are suspended and new ones appear — impossible, unpredictable things happen.

When the Redeemer comes close to men, even stranger things start happening. People who have hated him all their lives suddenly find a strange, mysterious love for this God and they fall at his feet. Paul, a man who hated Christ and all Christians, who breathed murderous threats against the whole Church, found himself broken when Jesus came close to him. For thousands of years men and women have come face to face with the God they once thought didn't exist, and they were shaken to the roots by the experience.

When the Lord of the Church comes close to his people, really impossible things begin to happen! You can read of times like this in the history of the Church — they are called "revivals" — when all the bickering, backbiting, finding fault, secret sins, politics, apathy, love of the world, and all sorts of stupidity suddenly stop and the whole place looks like a scene out of Heaven itself. People who used to never get along, now love each other — they laid aside their grievances and "consider others better than themselves." Instead of talk about baseball games, they can never get enough of hearing about Christ – not just from the sermons but from each other during the week! What's the difference? It is this: the Lord again sits among his people, on his throne, and they gather around him, arm in arm, in worship and praise. One would think that it could never happen, and yet there it is.

There is something about the nature of God that, when he is near, things change. Nothing and nobody stay the same in his presence. It may be for good or for ill, but it's guaranteed that the action will begin when the Lord shows up.

Actually we can pull out all the Names of God and use them to illustrate the glory of God. Have you ever tried to imagine what the "Deliverer" looks like? Do you have any idea what would happen if he suddenly showed up in the middle of his enemies – people that you and I know, who hate God and anything that has to do with Christian faith? They would be terrified! He would tramp through them like treading grapes; it is a fearful image of something that God actually does to human souls. Or what if he took hold of you, just when you thought all your problems were pulling you under in despair, and lifted you out into peace and protection? You don't have to imagine it — he does this for people, just like he did it for David, as we have recorded in Psalm 18. David was awe-struck with the reality of God's wrath – he *really does* destroy sinners — and the reality of God's profound love for his people. David loved to see God in action in this world.

The Lord is full of glory whether anybody knows it or not. He existed long before there was such a thing as time, long before the world existed, long before there were angels and men capable of seeing his glory. He doesn't need anybody to tell him about his glory — he knows what he is. But now *we* need to see it. That's the reason the Bible talks so much about his glory. God has various ways of grabbing our attention and making us see that there is a God in Heaven, that he is doing things in our lives that we need to be aware of, that he is a help and a resource that we need to start using for a change. He uses Creation to convince us of his power and wisdom and infinite resources; he uses history to teach us that he has everything under control; he uses the testimony of people here and there to bring the reality of Heaven close to us — this stuff actually happens to ordinary men and women that we know!

> Therefore, since we are surrounded by such a great cloud of witnesses, let us throw off everything that hinders and the sin that so easily entangles, and let us run with perseverance the race marked out for us. (Hebrews 12:1)

Since the beginning of the world, the Lord has made a massive effort to bring his Name and his reality under our noses so that we would be convinced that he isn't just a story. This has been the biggest advertising campaign, so to speak, in the history of the universe. Everywhere we see God's billboards screaming in big letters that God exists! That he is the maker of all this. That he gives life and defeats all forms of death. And that he is here, among us, holding the forces of evil at bay single-handedly in order to give us a chance to break through the line and burst over onto God's side where it is safe. If we don't know any of this, it's because we have our eyes shut and we can't see the Lord's billboards.

WHY MUST WE KNOW?

As we study about the Lord's glory we find that he is extremely jealous about it. "I am the LORD; that is my Name! I will not give my glory to another or my praise to idols." (Isaiah 42:8) He doesn't want any rivals. Whatever he is, he wants it made plain that nobody else and nothing else can do what he can do; he is the only place where you will find light and life and peace. Whenever someone else claims to give you what your soul needs, that god is an impostor.

But with all the false gods running around in our day, the knowledge of the true God — the God of the Bible — is almost drowned out! Nobody wants to hear anymore what the Bible has to say about God; fewer and fewer people darken the doors of churches, and ignorance of the truth is spreading rapidly, and the few Christians that are left are fighting for their lives, so to speak, in the public debates on religious and moral issues. Everyone seems to be an expert on God (though they don't have any idea of what the Bible says about him): whether he exists or not, what he is like if he does exist, and what our relationship is with him, if any. Unfortunately the conclusions that most people are coming up with are far from the truth.

We must find the *true* God. Only the God of the Bible can solve man's enormous problems, and only the God of Abraham, Isaac, and Jacob can raise the dead from their graves and reverse the curse of sin on men's souls. Though modern man seems content with his gods, they cannot help him in the day of death — or in the day of disaster either, for that matter, which keeps coming around in history and sweeping civilizations away from the scene. Our only hope for stopping the destruction that tears down both men and nations is to find a God who sits far above all the turmoil of the world.

That's why the news must get out that there *is* such a God and he *can* save from sin and death. At first people will be skeptical about the news; but God is different from any other god — he backs up the news about him with glory. When he demonstrates his reality, there isn't any more skepticism.

- *God's glory differentiates him from any other god.* People may have a lot of mistaken notions about who God is and what he does, but when he finally shows his glory then they get their opinions abruptly changed to fit the facts. They may reject what they see, but they *are* going to see the truth about God!

    When Moses went to Pharaoh demanding that the Israelites be set free, Pharaoh scoffed at the demand. He thought he knew about all these local gods, including Moses' Yahweh! And he figured he had nothing to worry about. So they had a contest — a war of the gods — in which Moses set out to prove that his God was much different from anything Pharaoh had ever seen in any of his gods. For a while they were running head to head — Yahweh turned the Nile into blood, and then the magicians turned it to blood too by the help of their gods; Yahweh brought a plague of frogs, and the magicians did the same thing. But soon Yahweh pulled out ahead and started doing things that the magicians couldn't do — and Pharaoh started worrying. "This is the finger of God," his magicians told him. (Exodus 8:19) And then the Lord started doing things to Egypt that positively alarmed Pharaoh — not safe little tricks to impress him but damaging things to ruin him. Flies ruined the land! Livestock died; people got boils; hail beat down their grain; locusts ate what was left; darkness settled over the land. And then came the disaster that broke Pharaoh's stubbornness and sent him sprawling before the only God in abject fear: the deaths of the firstborn of all the households of the Egyptians. When God was done with Pharaoh he knew there was a God here that was unlike any other god he had ever seen or imagined. The others weren't really gods compared to this one.

When God glorifies himself, he does it in such a way that convinces people that here is a God who does things that nobody else can do. He does the impossible! He does eternal things. He touches the soul, where no other god can reach, and saves from sin. He lifts up his people above the turmoil of the world into his kingdom where no principality or power can ever reach, where there is no more death or tears or sin, where there are no more thieves or rust or moth to corrupt. This God is able to make good on claims that other gods, other hopes that men look to for help, wouldn't dare to claim, let alone try. Remember the showdown between Baal and Yahweh on Mt. Carmel? It was Elijah who suggested the test — fire falling down from Heaven and burning up the sacrifice. In fact, he made it even more interesting by dowsing his own sacrifice in gallons of water! And the Israelites found out that day, because God glorified himself, that Yahweh exists and he does what no other god could dream of doing.

• *God's glory offers real hope of salvation.* People don't understand the predicament that sin has us under until the negative side of sin starts working on their lives. While the fun lasts they give no thought at all to their souls; but when the seamier side of sin gets hold of them then they start suffering. For a while, we buy whatever we want from the world and the devil; but then the day comes when we have to pay — and we end up paying dearly. Our present society is living proof of that. Almost half of all marriages self-destruct, teenagers destroy their minds and bodies on dope, crime runs rampant in every city and town, murder and rape are at all-time highs, the economy runs wild, the courts routinely let offenders go back into society free, churches split and proliferate on hatreds and die every week — on and on we could go. Because we as a nation have turned away from God and his truth, he has turned away from us — and the results are truly frightening. Things could be a lot worse, but that's small consolation for the troubles that we have on our hands right now.

In the middle of the ruinous disaster that sin brings down on our heads, the Lord sometimes displays his glory — a glory that proves that he is able and willing to save any sinner from any predicament that they've gotten themselves into. Perhaps the most touching and the most convincing example of this is the story of the adulterous woman whom the Pharisees brought to Jesus for condemnation. You know the story: she was caught in adultery, her accusers hauled her off to Jesus to ruin both her and him (they were using her to trap him too) and they demanded that Jesus condemn her to death. She didn't have much reason to hope, did she? But with a few words from the Master she was completely delivered from her accusers, forgiven of all her sin against God, and sent away with God's blessing on her head. One minute she was as good as dead with no hope, and literally the next minute she was free and assured of Heaven. (John 8:1-11)

There are many testimonies of people in the Bible and in the Church who have found God's power of salvation to be very real. They remember the struggles under sin that they once had, that old taskmaster that forced their noses into the ugliness of lusts and greed and pride and rebellion. They had no hope of ever escaping such a life; in fact, they had little idea of what life would be like apart from their sin. But God reached down from Heaven, took hold of their hearts and shook them free from the chains that bound them to sin and death and brought them into life and light. They are changed people now – "born again" in the full sense of that phrase — who are utterly convinced of the reality of God and his ability to save. There are many people who praise God because of this glory of his — they experienced it first hand.

• ***His glory overshadows our glory.*** As we saw at the beginning of this chapter, man is all too prone to stick himself out front in order to get the attention. But that doesn't last when God shows up — there are many examples of this in the Scriptures. People fall on their faces in front of God; they aren't even able to stand on their feet before him unless he lifts them up. They are ashamed and confused; they fear what he sees in their hearts and what he might do to them. They are so terrified that they would rather be anywhere else in the world than here, so close to Power and Truth, where one's soul could be unmade. And even this won't happen unless God *lets* them get near to him and live to tell about it — usually men die at the sight of God! (Exodus 33:20)

John the Baptist knew that Jesus' glory far outshone anything he himself was doing for God's kingdom. "He is the one who comes after me, the thongs of whose sandals I am not worthy to untie." (John 1:27) That wasn't false humility on his part: he knew that the Messiah was God, that he was pure and righteous and holy, that he had the power of the Spirit to change men's hearts and deliver them from death to eternal life. John could do nothing compared to Jesus:

> I baptize you with water for repentance. But after me will come one who is more powerful than I, whose sandals I am not fit to carry. He will baptize you with the Holy Spirit and with fire. His winnowing fork is in his hand, and he will clear his threshing floor, gathering the wheat into his barn and burning up the chaff with unquenchable fire. (Matthew 3:11-12)

So John stepped out of the limelight. I wish more preachers would have the spirit of John the Baptist! John announced the presence of the Christ, stepped aside, and was perfectly content to watch the Lord deal with his own people and get the credit. And John's attitude was entirely proper concerning the Lord: "He must become greater, I must become less." (John 3:30) John wasn't able to help anybody, not to the extent that people needed in order to be saved and to learn of God; only Jesus can do that for us. The proof is easy to see in the results of each of the men's ministries: John preached and they were impressed; Jesus preached and they were healed, changed, saved. Christ used this very point to convince John that he was the Messiah. (Matthew 11:1-6) God's glory outshines man's glory like the sun outshines a candle; the proof is in what it does.

• ***God's glory will triumph.*** Though men have all sorts of gods and mistaken opinions about the true God, all that will one day change when God comes to judge the whole world. For now he tolerates men's sins; instead of forcing everyone to see him as he really is, he lets them go on in their ignorance — he even lets them say things about him that are downright blasphemous! Right now is the day of salvation; he is working to bring his people into the kingdom of Heaven, and instead of running the risk of "tearing up the wheat with the weeds" he allows the weeds to grow.

But someday that will change. He promised us that at the end of time he will get all the glory that is due to him — everyone will finally see who he is, that he is the only God, that he really did make this world and provide for all of their needs, that he really was the source of all good, that his Truth really was the only way of looking at reality, that he really was their only hope if they wanted to be saved, and that he really is the Judge who is about to decide their eternal fate. All this will be made very plain on that day.

> Look, he is coming with the clouds, and every eye will see him, even those who pierced him; and all the peoples of the earth will mourn because of him. So shall it be! Amen. (Revelation 1:7)

Many people think that such a thing will never happen. But they shouldn't mistake God's present patience as a permanent radio silence; that day is coming, even more surely than the rising of the sun:

> The Lord is not slow in keeping his promise, as some understand slowness. He is patient with you, not wanting anyone to perish, but everyone to come to repentance. But the Day of the Lord will come like a thief. The heavens will disappear with a roar; the elements will be destroyed by fire, and the earth and everything in it will be laid bare. (2 Peter 3:9-10)

On that day the Lord will unleash the full power of his glory and the sight of it will begin the next chapter of God's works: eternity. All flesh will bend their knees before the Lord Almighty — even those hardened rebels who have had no love for God and his Son:

> That at the Name of Jesus every knee should bow, in Heaven and on earth and under the earth, and every tongue confess that Jesus Christ is Lord, to the glory of God the Father. (Philippians 2:10-11)

And once they have all bowed their knees to him in complete surrender, he will separate the righteous from the unrighteous and send them off to their respective homes forever. Finally, what we Christians have been hoping for all these thousands of years will happen — all wrongs will be made right, all injustices will be dealt with, the wicked will get what they deserve, the righteous will get what they have been hoping for in Christ, and God's glory will shine over all without a single cloud to obscure it.

PRAYING FOR HIS GLORY

Perhaps there is no more important thing to pray for than the glory of God. All the other "essentials" seem to converge on this one point. We read about God's nature in the Word — wouldn't it be great if it became real in our lives? The Spirit brings us into God's presence — wouldn't it be wonderful to see God become real on earth? And his names — they all describe a God that we need now, someone who will really do these things for us.

When we pray, we are supposed to pray in faith — that spiritual ability to see the reality of God's world and lay hold of it, in spite of the impossibility of it. Will he reward our faith and turn our problem-filled world inside out with answers from Heaven? We pray for his will, not ours — and his will is that his kingdom might extend to every human being and every activity on earth. Will we ever see such a kingdom?

Being Christians, we believe in all of this. But now it's time to pray for it to happen! The time is long overdue for the glory of God to reassert itself over us and the rest of the world. We should be praying that these things would happen:

> • *For things that only God can do.* Remember that faith lays hold of the impossible, the things that God promised in the Bible but that nobody believes can happen. We pray for God's glory when we pray for such things. Who will be impressed when we pray for what any god could deliver? Will the world want to switch gods if our God can't do any more than its false gods can? If our God can't produce hard evidence for his existence, then who will believe in him?
>
> I think that this is the root problem of the Church today. What goes on in most congregations are events that are easily explained by the world under well-understood categories. Ministry is often only the same counseling principles that the world discovered and wrote up in textbooks a couple of decades ago; we are just behind the times, that's all. We aren't doing anything in that area that the world itself hasn't been doing for quite a while. Furthermore, we talk about Heaven and the kingdom of God, but what the world sees are the riches of this world, not spiritual riches, and the will of man, not God's will. And we call Jesus the Lord, but we hold up men in his place and honor them instead and follow whatever they tell us — even when (incredibly!) it goes against the Lord's Word.
>
> What we need right now are some old-fashioned miracles for a change. We need things to happen that will make unbelievers stop in their tracks, blinking their eyes in unbelief, unable to

explain what they saw with any of their natural categories. We need things to start happening that will make people say, "That couldn't have happened! This is the finger of God!" Not the ordinary, run-of-the-mill stuff that the world is used to seeing from us, but things that only God can do – things that beggar the imagination. We need to pray for the blind to receive sight, for the lame to walk, for those who are sick to be healed, for the deaf to hear, for the dead to be raised, and for the poor to hear the good news. Now you could pray for these things to happen on the physical level, but why not go all out and pray for the really impossible — that the spiritually blind would see God, that the spiritually lame would walk in God's ways, that those who are dead to him would wake up and find themselves in his presence? When you pray for this to happen, you are asking for God's glory to descend to the earth and form the eternal kingdom that Heaven is made of. That will open some eyes!

• *That he might be in our midst.* Christians seem content to be away from home, for some reason. What I mean is this: it appears that we are on earth, and God is in Heaven, and that's the way things are. Prayer brings us close to God for a short time, but then we have to come back to earth and live our ordinary lives.

But didn't God promise us better than that? He said that he would live among us — right here where we are — and walk with us and talk with us. He leads us like a shepherd; he teaches us his ways and instructs us in the way to live. He feeds us daily. It's true that we go to him in worship; but it's no less true that he comes back *with* us to face the world. "I will never leave you or forsake you." "I will be with you always, to the very end of the age." "I will not leave you alone."

Now what kind of life do you think you will have when God himself walks with you? It can't be an ordinary life! You are going to look very much different than others around you. You're going to do things that they would never think of doing, and you are going to avoid the sin that they enjoy. Your tastes will be completely different. They aren't going to understand you at all!

> Live such good lives among the pagans that, though they accuse you of doing wrong, they may see your good deeds and glorify God on the day he visits us. (1 Peter 2:12)

In other words, it will be obvious to them that God has a firm hold on your life. That's the kind of testimony that you should pray for — because God covers you with his glory.

And this especially holds true for the Church itself. If there is any place on earth where it ought to be apparent that God is real, it's in the Church. There need to be some drastic changes in the Church before this will happen, but we simply have to pray for it — it's too important to overlook. Where the people of God gather together, there the Lord will be — that's his promise. And like a King seated on a throne with all his people gathered around before him, or like a Father with all his children at his knees, the people of God should have their eyes and hearts fully focused on the Lord when they come together in his Name. And it won't be their imaginations, either: the Lord will be there in power, in heavy reality, charging the spiritual air with visions of Heaven and praises of the saints and the conviction of hearts made bare in his presence.

> But if an unbeliever or someone who
> does not understand comes in while
> everybody is prophesying, he will be
> convinced by all that he is a sinner
> and will be judged by all, and the
> secrets of his heart will be laid bare.
> So he will fall down and worship
> God, exclaiming, "God is really
> among you!" (1 Corinthians 14:24-
> 25)

That's the kind of church service you should
pray for.

• *That we will see his glory better.* It's entirely
possible that God will display his glory and we will
miss it! It takes "eyes to see and ears to hear" —
physical eyes and ears won't pick up the things of
God. That's one of the reasons that God gives new
life, a new *kind* of life, to his children, so that they
can experience the reality of Heaven. Otherwise
they will never see it. (John 3:3)

But just because you have been made alive
to God doesn't mean that you will see all of his
glory. There are many obstacles in the way, and
Christians are subject to them too. Our faith falters
because the mountains of problems look too big to
solve; we lose hope because we believe the lies of
those who want to discourage us; our own sin
clouds up the view of God's blessings; humdrum
daily activities make us think that God's kingdom is
on hold for the time being.

You should pray, then, that God would
glorify himself in your eyes. You need it. You
need the daily reminder that God is here with you.
You need the constant encouragement of the
presence of the Almighty, the Father, the Shepherd,
the Refuge. You need God's answers, his treasures,

not your continuing problems and the empty husks of the world. If you are one of those who are willing to live on bread and water, then you will continue to pray for low-level answers that won't strengthen your soul — those people pray for physical blessings because they are either afraid of the treasures of Heaven or they don't realize that they could be living on a much higher plane than they are. But if you are one of those who aren't satisfied with anything less than the best, then pray for the best: pray for his glorious wealth and power. "Set your minds on things above, not on earthly things." (Colossians 3:2)

If you pray like this, God will honor that prayer, and your life will turn into a testimony that honors God and brings glory to him. The brighter you burn, the better that others will see Jesus in you. If there is only a smoldering coal in your heart, a trace of a spiritual life but nothing that makes you remarkably different from others, then that's not much of a testimony; people aren't going to be convinced that living with God makes a difference. But when our lives are wrapped in the flames of the Spirit and we live in two worlds, people stand in awe and think, "Surely this person walks with God!"

• *That we might become less.* Here is the tough part. In order for the glory of God to shine the brightest, we have to get out of the way of the light. God must get the credit for things, not us.

> Do not think of yourself more highly than you ought, but rather think of yourself with sober judgment, in accordance with the measure of faith God has given you. (Romans 12:3)

What skills do you have except those God has graciously given you? What have you accomplished in life except those things that God carefully prepared and blessed so that they would succeed for you? You think that you are righteous and holy, but remember the time when God found you "kicking in your blood," a helpless victim to your sins? Yes, you have a title to Heaven, but remember the Savior who bought that title for you with his precious blood. Whatever you are, and whatever you have, you owe completely to God.

There's no shame in that. What do you think your own efforts and accomplishments would do for you in eternity? God's works make your life worth living here because of their infinitely greater value than your own works; he is that good at what he does. It's like the difference between a master craftsman and his apprentice: the apprentice shouldn't grudge his master's greater skill — he should value it as something that will help him. In the same way, the preciousness of Heaven is based on God's greater skill and wisdom; we couldn't do nearly as good a job at it as he does.

The proper attitude is the one Jesus told us to take:

> Suppose one of you had a servant plowing or looking after the sheep. Would he say to the servant when he comes in from the field, "come along now and sit down to eat"? Would he not rather say, "Prepare my supper, get yourself ready and wait on me while I eat and drink; after that you may eat and drink"? Would he thank the servant because he did what he was told to do? So you also, when you have done everything you were told to do, should say, "We are unworthy servants; we have only done our duty." (Luke 17:7-10)

If you want to do this right, you will find it virtually impossible to pull off. There are just too many ways that we can make ourselves look good at the Lord's expense, and it gives us pain to think of humbling ourselves, like servants, while the world watches. That's why we need to pray for the Lord's glory to overshadow ours; only God can help us do that.

For example, there are times when we are going to be slapped around by our enemies, but we have to "turn the other cheek" because we want to glorify God, not ourselves. This is his battle, he will take care of his enemies, and we are not allowed to "save face" by retaliating with our own strength. There are times when the world is going to challenge our faith with jeers and ridicule; we are not allowed to retaliate with a show of human reasoning and common sense and things that will appeal to their way of thinking — God demands that we "play the fool" and trust in what looks foolish. (1 Corinthians 1: 22-23)

When we pray for these kinds of things, we are praying for God's glory. We want to see him honored among men, especially among God's people, and we want to see him get the credit for what he has done. We want to bring people's attention to God. We want the Lord to move on the earth in such a way that people will know they have been visited by the Almighty.

AN EXAMPLE PRAYER

Hezekiah was one of the few kings of the southern kingdom of Judah who followed the Lord. The northern kingdom — Israel — had been hauled off into exile by the Assyrians, the country around Jerusalem was rapidly being eaten up by invaders, and Hezekiah and the remaining Israelites were holed up in and around the city waiting for the inevitable. It was only a matter of time before hungry Assyria turned its voracious appetite toward God's people again.

Finally the day arrived. Sennacherib sent his vast army out to surround Jerusalem, and the people stood along the walls looking out on a sea of hostile soldiers. The enemy commander stood in front of the gate and defied the God of Israel, saying this:

Who of all the gods of these countries has been able to save his land from me? How then can the LORD deliver Jerusalem from my hand? (2 Kings 18:35)

He went on and on about this, mocking the Israelites about their God. He figured that Yahweh couldn't do any more for them than the gods of other nations did for their peoples. Was he ever wrong!

Hezekiah, greatly distressed over this pagan ridiculing his God, went to pray:

O LORD, God of Israel, enthroned between the cherubim, you alone are God over all the kingdoms of the earth. You have made Heaven and earth. Give ear, O LORD, and hear; open your eyes, O LORD, and see; listen to the words Sennacherib has sent to insult the living God. It is true, O LORD, that the Assyrian kings have laid waste these nations and their lands. They have thrown their gods into the fire and destroyed them, because they were not gods but only wood and stone, fashioned by men's hands. Now, O LORD our God, deliver us from his hand, so that all kingdoms on earth may know that you alone, O LORD, are God. (2 Kings 19:15-19)

What Hezekiah was praying for was that God would glorify himself in front of this pagan, and also before his own people and the nations all around. The story goes on to say this:

That night the angel of the Lord went out and put to death a hundred and eighty-five thousand men in the Assyrian camp. When the people got up the next morning — there were all the dead bodies! So Sennacherib king of Assyria broke camp and withdrew. He returned to Nineveh and stayed there. (2 Kings 19:35-36)

This prayer needs almost no comment, and includes all the essentials that we've studied. He prayed in response to God's *Word* (which came through the prophet Isaiah.) He focused on the *Name* of God and saw him there in Heaven. He could see, by means of the *Spirit*, that God was the only true God — something that Sennacherib couldn't see. His *faith* took hold of the impossible and simply waited on God to do a miracle. He knew that God's *will* was to protect his people. He used all the essentials of prayer. But the overall point of his prayer was that God would come down and teach this unbelieving blasphemer a lesson that he could not mistake! The next morning it was plain to see that God had been there over the night; there was no way that the trapped Israelites could have wrecked such massive destruction, such wholesale slaughter, on the mighty Assyrian army. Sennacherib went home with his tail between his legs, beaten by a God he didn't think existed. And Hezekiah and the Israelites probably spent the next several weeks in wild rejoicing because their God came in power and delivered them by his own hand — something that hadn't happened since the days of David. It was a wonderful day for the people of God, and the Lord got himself glory that day.

SUGGESTED PRACTICE

You should go back over the previous lessons and review the other essentials of prayer. They all come together here, as you have probably seen, and if you have a good understanding of the other five points then you can more easily understand how to pray for God's glory.

Perhaps you should start by finding out why your life is so drab and uninteresting! Living with God is thrilling. It may not always look thrilling on the outside, but then we live in two worlds at the same time. Here we eat and work and plan and suffer and enjoy the fruit of the world, just like everyone else; but spiritually we live in the light of God's presence, and that means that we will see God's glory in our lives. He will do things that we can't possibly do, and he will work in such a way that will cause others to wonder what we have inside us.

Another thing that you should do is find out what may be in your life that gets in the way of God's glory. Remember that we are desperate for attention, for getting credit, for appearing to be more than what we really are. We don't like to play the fool for anybody. But when it comes to God, we *must* play the fool. "If any one of you thinks he is wise by the standards of this age, he should become a fool so that he may become wise." (1 Corinthians 3:18) Paul isn't telling us to become idiots; he is saying, however, that when we submit to God in all things, including turning over all glory and credit to him alone, the world isn't going to understand that. They do things to draw attention to themselves; they don't understand someone who crucifies himself and lifts up Jesus in his place.

CONCLUSION

We have covered a lot of material in this study on prayer, much more than just the "six essentials." Probably we have touched on most of the things that one could say about prayer. But you must realize that this study was not intended in any way to be an exhaustive survey on prayer. Many issues were only mentioned in passing; many were not studied in depth because that wasn't the purpose of this particular study. So if you feel like something was missing, it probably was – intentionally so. As was said at the beginning, there are many good books on prayer that deal with other facets of the subject.

The purpose of this study was to focus on six problem areas. It seems as if these six things are difficult for Christians to master, especially in our modern age. The temptations and threats of our present society seem to be particularly dangerous for this kind of praying. If conditions change, and history shows that they usually do in time, then perhaps there will be other things about prayer that become more difficult and these six will be easier. For instance, before the modern critical age it wasn't a problem to pray according to God's Word because Christians simply believed whatever it said, as it stood, without any reason to doubt it. Now, however, our scientific, social, and psychological sophistication make it hard to swallow without a great deal of twisting and turning to make it say what we want it to say. Maybe in the next century the Christians will return to their simple faith in the Bible and pray for what it says.

I know that this is tough stuff. This is not milk for babes, but meat and potatoes. Instead of comforting you with the nice things that God will do for you in answer to your prayers, I challenged you with your possible failure to pray as God wants you to pray. There are times when we need encouragement, but then there are times when we have to look at the situation and shore up sagging timbers. You must realize that God is involved in prayer just as much as you are; not only should we look at what *we* get from prayer, but we should look at what *God* wants from it too. This study has focused on God's side, primarily, and worked backwards to our side: if *this* is what God is like, then *this* is how we should pray. There are requirements, you know, for serving God acceptably. The job that we have to do is just too big to go about it wrong.

Don't lose heart, however. If you are really the Lord's child then he won't leave you stranded with things that you can't possibly do. He is determined to train you in his ways, to give you spiritual skill to do the work of Heaven, to equip you with his weapons and his tools. You will find that, as you keep coming to him — perhaps helplessly, not knowing what to say or do, but that doesn't matter — he stands ready to help you obey him in all things. Practice makes perfect, they say. The more you pray, the more familiar you will get with the things of God, the more comfortable you will get with God, and — this is the bottom line, remember — the more answers you can expect.

APPENDIX: SIX OBJECTIONS ANSWERED

Prayer isn't the easiest thing in the world to do. If you find prayer to be easy, perhaps you are missing some of its more important aspects; the problems that we encounter in this world will crush us if we don't find answers in God's spiritual world, and the realities of God's world are impossible to see and get hold of without God's help. We are in the middle: somehow we have to get out of this world of sin and death, and we have to get into God's world of life and righteousness. It's an impossible situation without the Spirit.

People who take prayer lightly, as if it's an easy thing to do, don't understand what is going on when someone prays. Who would have been more skilled at prayer than our Lord Jesus? And yet, when he prayed, he struggled with all his strength, and "his sweat was like great drops of blood falling on the ground." (Luke 22:44) People in the Bible cried when they prayed; they pleaded with God and struggled with him. Jacob wrestled with the angel of God all night. (Genesis 32:32) Paul went back three times to plead with God about his problem — an *apostle* who could heal people of their sicknesses! (2 Corinthians 12:7-10) In Romans we find that, far from being easy, we often don't know what we should say when we pray; no less a power than the Holy Spirit has to step in and show us what to say. (Romans 8:26-27) David fasted and prayed for seven days concerning his baby son. (2 Samuel 12:15-23)

So prayer is difficult, and you should expect it to be. Jesus told us that the kingdom of Heaven is precious and we should be ready to sell all we have to buy it (Matthew 13:44-46); and men of strength and courage are fighting their way into it. (Matthew 11:12) Anything that is as precious and valuable as the kingdom of God is worth struggling for; and considering the opposition that we are going to get from all kinds of directions — not the least of which is our own hearts – this is going to be warfare all the way.

But these "six essentials" seem to make prayer ten times more difficult than it already is! Many people who work through this material get totally discouraged; they feel that they can't pray anymore, or at least they feel self-conscious about their prayers, and that interferes with what they are trying to say.

I don't mean to burden poor Christians with impossible conditions and keep them away from their Heavenly Father with "rules and regulations" made by men. Prayer should be the most precious experience that you have in life. You should be able to come to your Father about any concern and talk it over freely with him; you have that right as a child of God. The way you pray shouldn't be a stumbling block to your prayers.

On the other hand, there are some important considerations about God that you must admit are true. We want prayer to be good and encouraging and fruitful; but we shouldn't expect to buy that at the price of replacing God with a false god. If God is really what the Bible says he is, then that means we have to pray a certain way if we want him to listen to us.

I've taken a different approach to the subject than the average book on prayer would normally take: normally a book would look at the different functions of prayer (intercession, praise, confession, request, and so on) and work upward to God — in other words, start with what we have to do and what, therefore, we can expect God to do. This study, however, starts at the top and works down: I've looked at divine realities (the nature of God's Word, the work of the Spirit, the nature of God's Name, the gift of faith, the will of God and the glory of God) and worked down to our level — if this is what God looks like, how then should we pray? What difference does it make how we pray and what we say, when we know that God is like such and such? When you take this approach you stand a better chance of getting it right. When you start with man, you tend to accept what man is and does, and then when you get to God you often have to adjust what God looks like and what God does in order to fit in with the works and expectations of man. But when you start with God, you get your facts about him right in the beginning, and then you find out how man has to fit in with God's requirements.

These six points also seem to cause a substantial amount of pain and consternation. People get uncomfortable when they pray; they worry about whether they are saying the right thing to God; they are afraid to pray for fear that they will do something wrong. They get discouraged, and sometimes they get upset at the seemingly unnecessary rules and chuck the whole thing. Of course this isn't good; prayer shouldn't be a pain but a joy.

When this happens, though, it often means that the doctor has put his finger on the source of the trouble. When you are sick and at the doctor's office, he keeps poking around on your chest and stomach and asking you, "Does this hurt? Does it hurt here?" Then he presses one place and you yelp in pain; he doesn't have to ask anymore because he knows he found the problem.

When the Holy Spirit probes around in your heart he is going to put his finger on the problem area and you are going to hurt. Now some people don't like to hurt, physically or spiritually; they will do whatever it takes to avoid hurt. The problem is that they would sooner die than be healed! God doesn't make you hurt because he enjoys it; he hurts you (not maliciously, but probingly) in order to locate the problem. When he finds that problem he is always ready with the medicine, however; he will never leave us in our pain with no hope. The medicine may be bitter, the splint may make us hurt even worse, or he may take up a sharp scalpel in order to forcibly cut the problem out of us; but his intention is to heal us, not hurt us.

If there is any truth in these "six essentials" (and it's up to you to search the Scriptures to see if they are true) then don't be surprised if your prayer life immediately suffers. When we turn the lens on God and focus it better, so that we see him more clearly, then the light from his glory is going to show up the flaws in our own nature more clearly; it's inevitable. If we adjust our understanding of God to better fit the truth, then don't be surprised to find that you had some details wrong in the beginning. It shouldn't make us miserable to understand God better! If you have to change some of your ways to fit the realities of Scripture, then praise God that he showed you the truth — otherwise you would have continued in your ways of doing things completely ignorant of the fact that you weren't getting anywhere with God. Don't you appreciate it when people tell you the truth about yourself? (Though it might hurt!) As the Scripture says, "The kisses of an enemy may be profuse, but faithful are the wounds of a friend." (Proverbs 27:6) If you have bad breath, spiritually speaking, then it's best to find out so that you won't continue to offend others with it — especially when it's God that you are trying to please.

Nevertheless, we ought to look at six common objections to these essentials of prayer. Many people, when they first hear these points, will say in objection:

You're making me feel uncomfortable when I pray.

If that means that you are finally looking at what you say and how you say it, then good! There's nothing wrong with feeling uncomfortable if you are doing something wrong. In fact, it's a good thing that you feel uncomfortable about it – you will more likely change what you are doing, if it's wrong, in order to satisfy God's requirements. A lot of people are hardened to the truth, and they don't care whether they are doing prayer correctly, and they will never look into it. But when something disturbs a conscientious person then he will probably try to find out what is wrong; it's only when we are happy and unconcerned that nothing gets changed.

You shouldn't always be uncomfortable, however. The idea is to get better at this business, not remain an amateur at it. A beginning athlete almost always feels awkward when he does what his coach tells him. But a professional is well trained; the right moves are somehow part of him now, and they come naturally. He doesn't even think about how he does it because it happens on its own — because of the long years of sweat, labor, tears, struggles, and pain. In order to become skillful at prayer, you must start at the beginning and train rigorously. You must learn the right words; you must practice obedience; you must study the Truth; you must kill the willfulness in your heart; you must come back after failure and failure until it starts working for you.

You are not alone in this. The reason that you have the Spirit of God in your heart is so that he can train you in the ways of God, including this matter of prayer. If you stay on the team and keep coming to practice, he will always, as a good coach, help you achieve your goal. You will have moments when you are discouraged and feel like giving up; then the Spirit will encourage you with the hope that God has for you (like the prize at the end of the race!), and promise you all the strength and skill that he possesses to help you win the race.

I don't think that God wants me to pay attention to such minute details.

As a matter of fact he requires much more detail than you could ever attend to in your prayers! If you need proof of this, refer to the laws concerning Temple worship in the Old Testament. It seems as if some of those laws were totally unnecessary – like silver spikes and purple weavings and horns on the altar. Yet every detail of the Temple was so important to God that, if one thing was missing, he would have stopped the whole proceeding until they fixed it!

The point is that every single detail means a great deal to God. The smallest requirement has infinite spiritual significance in the kingdom of God. Even though we may not know what it means spiritually, it *does* matter to him. Someday we will see how important all these "little details" were in the process of our salvation.

He hasn't burdened you with many of the necessary details, however. He has actually given you very little to do. Christ fulfilled, and continues to fulfill, the myriad of details that make up the entire worship of God. The process is so terribly complex that we wouldn't be able to figure it all out, let alone begin satisfying any of the requirements. Jesus, however, is the "great high priest" who is right now interceding with God on our behalf, offering up the sacrifice that will save us to the uttermost, offering up the correct prayers at the correct times that the ceremony demands. What *you* are left with is a small duty compared with what he is doing for you. "Take my yoke upon you ... for my yoke is easy and my burden is light." (Matthew 11:30)

Since your part is such a small portion of the work necessary to save you and to keep you in touch with Heaven, you shouldn't consider your work unnecessary. Don't let your pride lead you into thinking that your job seems so boring, so useless, that you want greater things to do. If you have been faithful in doing the little things then God will reward you with greater responsibilities, but if you despised the little things that he has given you to do, and slopped around on the details because you felt they were beneath you or weren't important, then don't expect God's approval of your work. A faithful workman will take care to attend to every single detail that relates to his work, not because he finds meaning in it (he may not!) but because he wants his boss's approval. A Christian should feel that way even more strongly, considering that his work is to help build the eternal kingdom of God. This work can't be done sloppily; there's too much that depends on the quality of the results.

It seems as if you are saying that I'm not allowed to pray about certain things.

That's not true. You can pray about anything that is on your heart. God will receive you concerning any issue in your life. The point isn't what you pray *about*, but what you pray *for*.

Where we inevitably go wrong is in what we want from God. There's nothing wrong with praying about food and drink and clothing; but Jesus' point in Matthew 6:25 was that life — Christian life — consists in *more* than these. Your cares should be where *your* battle is, not in how God does *his* job. Pray for your simple needs in the way that God told you to pray for them: he said he would provide you with what you need, so simply ask him to provide. No doubts, no worrying, no scheming on how you can increase your possessions and line your nest — just look to your Heavenly Father who knows you need the necessities of life and ask him for them. "Give us today our daily bread." (Matthew 6:11) Short and sweet. An unbeliever can't trust God to be that faithful about the necessities.

But what about the burdens that try our souls? There's nothing Christian about suffering (we all suffer), and there's nothing Christian about wanting to be comforted and encouraged during tough times. Everyone wants that! Everyone would like some encouraging words, an arm around the shoulder, a listening ear as we cry our heart out. But that's exactly the point — if that's all that we want, we can get that from anybody, not just from God! And if the only thing that is important to us is success in this world, then there are other ways of getting that success and smooth sailing without looking for answers in Heaven. Remember that Heaven and earth are opposites — Heaven is planning to destroy this world and all its "successes" and comforts! Heaven has a low opinion of what this world has to offer us.

When you have problems, then, pray about them — but look for the spiritual side that is involved. Your problems are for a purpose: to develop your soul in faith and love and holiness. Things that cause other people to jump off bridges should drive you to your Father who can give you what your soul needs. Problems and trials are the dinner plate upon which God heaps the bread of Heaven; they are opportunities for you to enter into your spiritual inheritance. I know that sounds crazy to an unbeliever; he wants problems solved in the world's way — more material goods, putting others down, a good feeling about himself, and so on. But when *you* come away from prayer, you will probably have nothing in your hands to show an unbeliever that prayer worked for you! In fact, your problems just may still be there – you may even get more problems! But what you got from God dazzled you; you don't care about the problems any more.

> Yet outwardly we are wasting away, yet inwardly we are being renewed day by day. For our light and momentary troubles are achieving for us an eternal glory that far outweighs them all. So we fix our eyes not on what is seen, but what is unseen. For what is seen is temporary, but what is unseen is eternal. (2 Corinthians 4:16-18)

We have to set our sights higher than this world. When others only want comfort and physical ease and success in the world's terms, we have to go for more – treasures that we can't have now, putting off success, being patient for justice, loving even when others hate us, believing even when it appears that all is hopeless. The kinds of things that we pray for would starve someone else; they can't live without the junk food that the world sells, whereas we live on a Heavenly diet that mystifies the unbeliever.

What you pray for shows what you are. If you ask for spiritual treasures then you prove that you are an heir of God. If you dig for the spiritual dimension in everything, then you demonstrate that you consider the spiritual worth digging for.

I feel as if God is glaring at me now.

No he isn't. He's your Father. He loves you with a love that staggers the imagination. He wants the best for you. He is helping you in this matter of prayer; he isn't sitting up there, arms across his chest, waiting for you to slip up. He sent the Spirit especially so that you can learn how to do this business in a way that will please him. He has given you every possible resource to teach you and train you, to supply you with whatever you may need. He has prepared all his spiritual treasures just for you, and he is ready to freely give. Like the prodigal's father, he stands with open arms ready to receive you.

But, nevertheless, he likes things done a certain way. What is wrong with that? Are you offended that he won't accept any craziness that might come out of your mouth? Are you going to insist on your own ways? Will you not change even if you know that God is offended with certain things that you do?

It's you who must change, not him. And it's not so humiliating to change for God's sake. Are you doing something that he doesn't like? At least you know now! At least he told you! He also told you how you can please him in every way, which is a great mercy; it proves that he loves us and he wants us to be near him. Your offense is on the scale of bad breath, not unforgivable sin. The only thing that will positively anger him is when you ignore his commands to change. He knows that you are a sinner, and he set up the necessary spiritual machinery to take care of your sin. You won't surprise him or change his mind about you when you sin against him. Just keep coming to him for his grace to cleanse your heart and make you into the image of Christ. You will always find him there with a wash-rag, so to speak, ready to mop up your dirty face, with no ill-will but plenty of love. What he cannot tolerate, however, is when you stubbornly hold to your own will. Then he *will* glare at you.

Shouldn't prayer be spontaneous and free, not burdened with all these heavy weights?

These "heavy weights" are God's guidelines to make your prayers more effective with him. If they are burdens to you, then perhaps you need to re-examine your foundations. When Jesus said that God requires those who worship him to worship in Spirit and in Truth — why do you consider it a burden to make sure that you pray in the Spirit and according to God's Truth? If Christ tells you that you haven't prayed for anything in his Name yet, why are you content to continue displeasing him in this way? If he wants you to pray for his will, why aren't you busy finding out what his will is? Is it a burden to you to obey the Lord? If so, you have reason to suspect your commitment to him.

There are certain things that are very important to God; he is more willing that the whole world would self-destruct than to see these things go undone. "I tell you the truth, until Heaven and earth disappear, not the smallest letter, not the least stroke of a pen, will by any means disappear from the Law until everything is accomplished." (Matthew 5:18) If you don't share his priorities then you need to do some serious soul-searching. What is important to God must become important to you, or you will be part of that world that he rolls up at the end of time and throws away as having served its purpose but has no part in eternity.

If you pass off the things that "burden" you when you pray, then you will have to forego the rewards as well.

The ordinances of the LORD are sure and altogether righteous. They are more precious than gold, than much pure gold; they are sweeter than honey, than honey from the comb. By them is your servant warned; in keeping them there is great reward. (Psalm 19:9-11)

The Pharisees thought that Jesus' teaching was too uncomfortable, that most of what he said was totally unnecessary. They found out that the heavy stone that they threw away was the only thing that could save them. "See, I lay a stone in Zion, a chosen and precious stone … the stone that the builders rejected has become the capstone." (1 Peter 2:6-7)

We will find that the burden, if we bring it to the Lord, will roll off our backs, and prayer done in God's way will become a delight and a precious time. The burdens will turn out to be our old sins: taking such pains as to pray in a way that pleases God 1) takes up too much of our time, 2) requires that I study the Bible for a change, 3) will mean that I must change what I want to do, and I will have to do what God wants me to do, and 4) (_fill in the blank!_) Bring those sins to the Lord to forgive and remove from your heart, and you won't call prayer a burden anymore.

What if I don't do all these things? Am I not praying?

Of course you are praying. Whenever you send up a request to Heaven, you are praying. _Who_ you are praying to may be a good question, and whether God is listening to you is another good question. Lots of people pray without giving any of these issues a single thought; but ask them if they get God's answers, and that will demonstrate that there is more involved here than just praying.

By God's grace his children will get blessed one way or another, and we can expect to get to Heaven on Christ's merits alone whether or not we prayed like spiritual adults. It is sort of like a nursery: mommies and daddies will love their babies and take care of their needs, but that's to be expected. What is alarming is when those babies grow up and keep goo-gooing and wetting their diapers and trashing the furniture around them. Babies are supposed to grow up and become adults, not remain babies. But if such monstrosities ever happen, the parents continue to care for their basic needs. So does God with his spiritual monstrosities that fill the nurseries that we call churches.

So you can continue to pray as you have always prayed, and you can expect to see God in Heaven someday. He isn't going to keep you out just because you weren't careful in how you prayed! The Spirit will make sure that, on occasion, you phrase a particular request in a way that prompts the Father to answer you. You may not realize what happened or why it happened, but God will take care of you one way or another by moving your heart to do it right once in a while.

My concern is that too many Christians are satisfied with living on a low level of spiritual maturity. We need men and women, not babies. The world is tearing itself apart right now with its God-hating, rebellious, self-destructive, wicked course; we need trained and skilled Christians to march into the devil's holocaust and rescue the perishing. The sad part is that the Church herself is largely to blame for the present condition of our society; Christians slid backwards in their spiritual walk with God, became impotent and ignorant, and sold their treasures to the enemy so that now we have no weapons to fight with and nothing outside of this world to cherish as worth living for.

Older generations always said that there are two things that will revive the Church and reform a society: the preaching of the Word (and that requires an unwavering faith in that Word as it stands) and prayer. Now I can't imagine that the prayers of the present day generation of Christians will ever reform our society; as a matter of fact, it *isn't* happening — things are getting worse. Something has to change. And my appeal is the same one that went out to Israel when David was wandering in the desert as an outcast and a criminal, as Jesus certainly is in our day: where are the men and women who understand the times and know what the people of God must do? (1 Chronicles 12:32) We desperately need the answers of God for our time — where are the Christians who will pray in such a way as to get those answers?

Notes

Other Titles From
Ravenbrook Publishers

Mystery Revealed: A Beginner's Bible Survey

Eight Fundamentals of the Christian Faith

No Proof Needed: The Bible is the Word of God

Jesus and the New Testament

The Witness

The Bible Explains Creation

Ten Keys to the Bible

Removing the Veil: What the Old Testament Is All About

www.ingramcontent.com/pod-product-compliance
Lightning Source LLC
Chambersburg PA
CBHW022130080426
42734CB00006B/295